"This book is a *tour de force* contribution to Gestalt therapy's theory of self. Macaluso addresses the original theory through a hermeneutic reading and with a critical evaluation of its various refinements over the last 75 years. He not only presents the original theory with a clarity that makes the book essential reading for students and practitioners at every level of experience, but his own critical approach is a significant contribution to Gestalt therapy's clinical phenomenology in its own right."

Dan Bloom, JD, LCSW, *President,* *New York Institute for Gestalt Therapy*

"Macaluso's wisdom glides us gracefully and respectfully, with clear and astute prose, through the developmental phases of the language and application of Gestalt therapy from beginnings to the present. I might have a different idea, here and there, but I would not hesitate to assign this book to interested students and practitioners. I was drawn in, captivated."

Lynne Jacobs, *Co-founder, Pacific Gestalt Institute Training analyst, Institute of Contemporary Psychoanalysis*

"I want to welcome this book by a senior Gestalt trainer to the recent writings about Self in Gestalt Therapy. He has brought together the original writing by Perls and Goodman with more recent contributions on the subject."

Peter Philippson, MSc, *Full Member, New York Institute for Gestalt Therapy, Founder Member, Manchester Gestalt Centre, Honorary Member, GPTI (UK), Founder Member, IG-FEST*

Phenomenology of the Self in Gestalt Therapy

Phenomenology of the Self in Gestalt Therapy is a compelling and insightful work that offers an original and in-depth perspective on Gestalt theory and practice.

With theoretical rigor and clear exposition, the author guides the reader through the core concepts of the model, such as the self, spontaneity, and contact, skillfully weaving together phenomenological reflection and clinical sensitivity. By revisiting the founding text of Perls, Hefferline, and Goodman in light of contemporary developments, Macaluso makes complex material accessible and reveals its ongoing relevance to therapeutic practice.

This is an essential text for psychotherapists, students, and scholars seeking to engage with the living heart of Gestalt and to deepen their understanding of how its theory can inform and enrich clinical work.

Mercurio Albino Macaluso is a clinical psychologist and Gestalt psychotherapist. He teaches at the Istituto di Gestalt HCC Italy and works within the public mental health service in Palermo. His research focuses on the phenomenology of the self and contemporary developments in Gestalt therapy theory and practice.

The Gestalt Therapy Book Series

Istituto di Gestalt

www.gestaltitaly.com HCC Italy

Series Editor **Margherita Spagnuolo Lobb**

The Istituto di Gestalt series of Gestalt therapy books emerges from the ground of a growing interest in theory, research and clinical practice in the Gestalt community. The members of the Scientific and Editorial Boards have been committed for many years to the process of supporting research and publications in our field: through this series we want to offer our colleagues internationally the richness of the current trends in Gestalt therapy theory and practice, underpinned by research. The goal of this series is to develop the original principles in hermeneutic terms: to articulate a relational perspective, namely a phenomenological, aesthetic, field-oriented approach to psychotherapy. It is also intended to help professions and to support a solid development and dialogue of Gestalt therapy with other psychotherapeutic methods.

The series includes original books specifically created for it, as well as translations of volumes originally published in other languages. We hope that our editorial effort will support the growth of the Gestalt therapy community; a dialogue with other modalities and disciplines; and new developments in research, clinics and other fields where Gestalt therapy theory can be applied (e.g., organizations, education, political and social critique and movements).

We would like to dedicate this Gestalt Therapy Book Series to all our mentors and colleagues who have sown fruitful seeds in our minds and hearts.

Coordinator
Stefania Benini

General Editor
Margherita Spagnuolo Lobb

For a full list of titles in this series, please visit www.routledge.com/Gestalt-Therapy/book-series/GESTHE and www.gestaltitaly.com

Titles in the series:

Enchantment and Gestalt Therapy: Partners in Exploring Life
Erving Polster

Exploring Masculinity, Sexuality, and Culture in Gestalt Therapy: An Autoethnography
Adam Kincel

Human Interaction and Emotional Awareness in Gestalt Therapy: Exploring the Phenomenology of Contacting and Feeling
H. Peter Dreitzel

Gestalt Therapy Practice: Theory and Experiential Learning
Gro Skottun and Åshild Krüger

The Relational Heart of Gestalt Therapy: Contemporary Perspectives
Peter Cole

The History, Theory and Community of Gestalt Therapy: Exploring the New York Institute
Václav Mikolášek

Psychopathology of the Situation in Gestalt Therapy: A Field-oriented Approach
Margherita Spagnuolo Lobb and Pietro Cavaleri

Relational Gestalt Therapy in India: A Guide to Group Practice
Vanaja Ammanath

A Field-Centred Approach to Gestalt Therapy: Agency and Response-ability in a Changing World
Lothar Gutjahr

A Gestalt Therapist's Guide Through the Depressive Field: Giving Way to Hope
Jan Roubal

Situation, Field Perspective and Formation of Forms in Gestalt Therapy: Social Change Begins with Two, 2e
Jean-Marie Robine

Gestalt Therapy in Times of War: New Clinical Tools and Political Consciousness
Edited by Margherita Spagnuolo Lobb, Pietro Andrea Cavaleri, Mattia Romano, and Giacomo Bisonti

Phenomenology of the Self in Gestalt Therapy: Individual and Field in the Therapeutic Situation
Mercurio Albino Macaluso

Phenomenology of the Self in Gestalt Therapy

Individual and Field in the Therapeutic Situation

Second Edition

Mercurio Albino Macaluso

Routledge
Taylor & Francis Group
LONDON AND NEW YORK

Designed cover image: Rolffimages by Dreamstime.com

Second edition published 2027
by Routledge
4 Park Square, Milton Park, Abingdon, Oxon, OX14 4RN

and by Routledge
605 Third Avenue, New York, NY 10158

Routledge is an imprint of the Taylor & Francis Group, an informa business

First edition published by FrancoAngeli 2023

British Library Cataloguing-in-Publication Data
A catalogue record for this book is available from the British Library

ISBN: 9781041213413 (hbk)
ISBN: 9781041213383 (pbk)
ISBN: 9781003726753 (ebk)

DOI: 10.4324/9781003726753

Typeset in Times New Roman
by Newgen Publishing UK

To my wife, Liana,
and to my children, Elena and Francesco

Contents

Preface

Margherita Spagnuolo Lobb[1]

In this book, Macaluso addresses the heated debate between individual and/or relational perspectives in psychotherapy, an issue that is at the center of the contemporary development of all "relational" approaches, and of course of Gestalt therapy. He achieves this by explaining the originality and uniqueness of the Gestalt perspective, with a hermeneutic analysis of the founding text, *Gestalt Therapy*, written by Perls, Hefferline, and Goodman in 1951. That text, as we know, was written using aesthetic categories that are not internalizable and with a deliberately complex language. Despite being a masterful integration of the cultural currents of the time and having the ability to stimulate new ideas and creativity in the reader, it has not made it easy for Gestalt therapists to find an epistemological framework in which to place their work. Macaluso, using clear language that closely aligns with the therapeutic relationship, accomplishes two important tasks with this book: first, he provides an extremely useful explanation of that text; second, he demonstrates that the individual and the relationship are two sides of the same coin. Thus, there is no distinct individual or relational Gestalt therapy; rather, the two perspectives were already perfectly integrated in the minds of the founders.

In phenomenological terms, reality is something we can only describe in the first person, that is, from a subjective perspective. However, individual subjectivity always emerges from a relationship (or a situational field) (Wollants, 2012; Spagnuolo Lobb, 2021) and carries with it the memory of this uniqueness. Without the situation from which subjectivity arises, subjective experience could not present itself to the world. Subjectivity and situation exist in a dynamic of mutual recognition and adaptation.

Who is Albino Macaluso? He is a senior trainer at the Institute of Gestalt HCC Italy, a scrupulous, profound, and kind professional, loved by all his students—a model of honest study of texts and a person of profound humanity. As he says in his introduction, Albino is also stubborn: if he has an idea, he pursues it over the years with determination and consistency, but never with arrogance or impulsivity. In his 30 years of teaching psychotherapy, he has always nurtured a passion for psychotherapeutic theory, particularly Gestalt therapy. He doesn't like to travel or seek the spotlight; what he writes and teaches comes from sincere dedication and rare intellectual honesty. For me, it has always been both an ethical duty and a pleasure to support his theoretical reflections and make them accessible to many, not just to the students of our school.

In addition to its theoretical and didactic value—how I wish my generation had access to such a text to understand the *Gestalt Therapy* (1951/1994), the foundational book!—this book fits into the culture of today's society, where the old diatribe between objective and subjective takes the form of an efficiency mentality that places pain and the patient's problem out there in an objective way. The model of "you have a problem: try to solve it" (which has made some influencers so successful) has taken hold among the youth, preventing them from pausing to reflect on the meaning of things or utilizing their sensations as a guide to solutions. Consequently, when they are hurt, they tend to either sink into depression or lash out violently at others. Drawing on phenomenology and aesthetics, Gestalt therapy proposes a model of knowledge that does not objectify the problem but experiences it firsthand, with the confidence that it is only by throwing oneself into life that one can orient oneself in it and solve the complexity of situations.

This book explains well how the epistemological transition from objectification to situated subjectification takes place, both in the founding text and everyday in the clinic. Both clinical examples and theoretical reasoning flow smoothly, without detracting from the complexity inherent in the Gestalt method.

The purpose of the book is to demonstrate that there aren't two Gestalt perspectives—one focused on the individual and one on the situation (or the field)—but rather that 'We speak of individual subjectivity for convenience, but the individual exists only within a shared field. Individual and relational dimensions are not separate—they constitute a single reality: the field' (p. 115).

The author demonstrates that, in the original formulation by the founders of Gestalt therapy, the individual and the field are not separated. Historical evolution initially favored the individual perspective, until the field perspective emerged strongly in recent years. However, this isn't a rupture or turning point; rather, it represents a deepening—a variation on the theme of an original idea.

The book is therefore a journey into the world of Gestalt, offering an explanation accessible to everyone, not just experts, about its core concepts and perspective on human beings and their relationships. The author invites us into this world, gradually revealing its language, its culture, where the concepts we read about in reference texts come from, and how they manifest in clinical practice. It is a coherent and profound world that is not simplistically identified only with the empty chair—although this technique remains extraordinarily innovative and revolutionary. It also integrates studies on perception from Gestalt psychologists, bodily processes, and movement, which are hallmarks of phenomenological depth. Additionally, it encompasses the emotions that emerge during the experience of contact, contributing to personality formation. The added value of this approach lies in its ability to make every therapeutic step and each attempt by the patient to confront life's difficulties feel poetic, thanks to its aesthetic language.

The *incipit*, the first chapter, analyzes the meaning and evolution of subjective experience in Gestalt therapy, exploring crucial aspects such as awareness, the present moment, surface experience, creative self-regulation, and the holistic nature of personal experience. It presents the key concepts of the Gestalt model (contact, contact-boundary, field), highlighting how they situate subjective experience within a relational and co-creative framework.

But the crux of the book lies in Chapter 2, where the author explains Paul Goodman's theory of the self and compares it with that of Isadore From. The clarity of this explanation is something I don't think I've ever encountered in any other writing, whether Italian or international. Beyond the clinical differences between these two entirely compatible versions, the novelty of the Gestalt self lies in its free, vital and spontaneous functioning,

> an experience that emerges when one is fully immersed in the present moment and in harmony with the environment. This state represents the essence of psychological health and the core of therapeutic work, which aims to discover the individual's creative potential and deepest resources
>
> (p. 32)

It is the particular "quid" that characterizes the self from a Gestalt perspective and explains the originality and effectiveness of its clinical interventions.

In the third chapter, the author distinguishes between the use of concentration to explore the patient's experience and the use of the therapist's spontaneity in order to work within a relational approach. We must not confuse spontaneity with impulsiveness. Spontaneity is the result of situated ethics, which take into account the situation and the other. In an era where the distinction between impulsivity and spontaneity is often unclear—such as when a politician, as a representative of the people, is forgiven for involvement in abuse or vandalism, or when there is little opposition to violence committed by those unable to tolerate frustration (as seen in femicides)—it is an ethical duty to teach that impulsivity stems from neurotic desensitization to others. In contrast, spontaneity is an art and a continuous exercise in moving while considering others and the situation, rather than merely an option.

In Chapter 4, the author discusses the integration of individual and relational perspectives. The clinical examples presented in this chapter, which illustrate the difference between relational work and relationship-centered work, seem masterful to me.

Chapter 5 delves, together with Chapter 6, into the experiential background, and is dedicated to the id. The author clearly describes the difference between the Gestalt id and the psychoanalytic id. The id is not, in fact, the unaware ground (a kind of unconscious), but rather the function of how the ground itself emerges. It's a way of functioning of the self. I find this chapter very beautiful, as it describes the richness and complexity of the concept of the "id" in Gestalt therapy, which is primarily responsible for the therapist's implicit intuition and the sense of intimacy that both the therapist and the patient achieve. If this reflection and description had been made at the time of Perls' death, it would certainly have prevented the caricatural spread of the founder's work, carried out by many therapists who imitated his deconstructive style without grasping its deeper meaning, subsequently disseminating a provocative and pedantic form of Gestalt therapy that has nothing to do with the "spirituality" underlying the concept of the id.

Letting yourself be transformed by the experience with the patient, without controlling or schematizing it, is not easy to learn. Students sometimes fear being overwhelmed by the patient's emotions, which makes it difficult for them to stay focused on their therapeutic task. For this reason, "the id can pave the way for a new model of psychotherapy, one that is aesthetic and intuitive, capable of considering also the deep and transcendent dimension of human experience" (p. 79).

Chapter 7, dedicated to personality—another type of experiential background—is theoretically intriguing and describes the originality of Gestalt therapy. The author highlights the need to address the background, as this enables the clinical shift from the exercise to modify the figure to the co-created field, to support, and to the restructuring of perceptual dynamics. The author achieves this through an original comparison between the studies of Gordon Wheeler and myself. This need, now made more urgent by the increased fragility of our patients, leads us to a Gestalt approach focused on support, rather than on deconstruction.

Chapter 8 is about the field. Fully aware of the various Gestalt interpretations of the field, the author does not intend to provide another definition but rather aims to contextualize the concept within its historical, cultural, epistemological, ecological, and phenomenological matrix, showing its development and the relevance of some of its aspects and connections today.

I have read and re-read this book a hundred times, with attention and care, discussing with the author every small detail that might not adequately consider the literature and international dialogues, while also allowing the author his own independent perspective, from which I sometimes diverge, to the benefit of the healthy debate that exists in our Institute. I feel that this care is reciprocated: with this book, he has also taken care of the theory I have developed, which has given rise to the model of our Institute. It is a wonderful feeling to be fully understood in one's teaching and to be "explained" to others through comparisons with the great figures of Gestalt therapy. I feel a deep gratitude toward Albino for weaving together the theoretical efforts of our Institute in silence, only to gift us this wonderful narrative of who we are in the international Gestalt evolution and the struggles we have endured to reach this milestone.

I hope this book is disseminated as it deserves, because it conveys the theoretical depth of Gestalt therapy and its importance in contemporary clinical practice, and because it does not create separations between different Gestalt approaches.

May all who read it feel captivated by Gestalt therapy!

Margherita Spagnuolo Lobb
Director Gestalt Institute HCC Italy

References

Perls, F., Hefferline, R., & Goodman, P. (1994). *Gestalt therapy: Excitement and growth in the human personality*. Highland, NY: The Gestalt Journal Press. (Original work published 1951).

Spagnuolo Lobb, M. (2021). Il lavoro sullo sfondo, l'estetica e la "danza": La conoscenza relazionale estetica e la reciprocità. In M. Spagnuolo Lobb & P. A. Cavaleri (Eds.), *Psicopatologia della situazione: La psicoterapia della Gestalt nei campi clinici delle relazioni umane* (pp. 25–48). Milano: FrancoAngeli.

Wollants, G. (2012). *Gestalt therapy: Therapy of the situation*. Thousand Oaks, CA: Sage. (Original work published 2008, Turnhout, Belgium: Faculteit voor Mens en Samenleving).

Note

1 Gestalt Institute Director HCC Italy.

Acknowledgments

I would like to thank all those who, in various ways, contributed to the creation of this book, acknowledging that the responsibility for any errors or omissions rests solely with me.

First and foremost, I am grateful to Margherita Spagnuolo Lobb, my teacher, who supported me in developing my personal vision of Gestalt therapy, offered me the opportunity to develop an international perspective, and guided me in the final drafting of all my articles.

I thank Piero Cavaleri, who, after reading my first article, encouraged me to continue writing, suggesting, prophetically, that I should eventually collect my works into a book. He also read the subsequent articles in advance, always offering valuable suggestions and insights.

I thank Betti Conte, Giuseppe Sampognaro, and Antonio Cascio for their timely and valuable feedback after carefully reading the drafts of some of my articles.

I thank Viviana Polizzi and Gina Merlo, dear friends as well as colleagues—first for reading each article in advance and receiving it with critical enthusiasm and second for our always passionate discussions on theory and clinical practice.

I thank my colleagues and friends from the Gestalt Institute HCC Italy for the ongoing dialogue and stimulating debate, which I have always considered a forge of ideas, reflections, and important insights for my profession, teaching, and writings.

I thank the students I have met during my teaching activities at the Institute. Through their questions and objections, they have encouraged my research and helped me refine my ideas.

I thank my sister Stefania, a philosophy teacher, for the intellectual stimulation I have always drawn from our exchanges and from her unique point of view.

Lastly, I thank Liana, my wife, for being the secure background that allowed the figure embodied by this book to emerge.

AI Acknowledgment

Chat GPT 5.1 was used throughout this book solely to translate and clarify the text from Italian to English—no ideas were generated by way of AI and all theoretical ideas and substantive content is that of the author.

Introduction

This book arises from a persevering, I would even say stubborn, reading of *Gestalt Therapy*, the fundamental text of Gestalt therapy, written by Perls, Hefferline, and Goodman and published in 1951. Over the years, I have become increasingly passionate about studying this text, which Gestalt therapists colloquially refer to as the "Bible." It is a work of astonishing richness in many respects, a treasure that unfortunately is little known because it is not easy to read. The section of *Gestalt Therapy* written by Goodman is, as Isadore From and Michael Vincent Miller (1994, p. ix) wrote in the introduction to the book's second edition, "a theoretical work written in uncompromisingly difficult prose". Goodman does not use the formal and abstract language typical of academic writings, but rather a vivid, plastic language that brings meanings to life through images and evokes experience in its concreteness. And he does it as a talented writer, mastering the linguistic registries. His writing style, dense and concise, does not lend itself to a hurried, superficial, and introjective reading. His complex reasoning develops recursively. Many concepts are first anticipated, sometimes in an almost hermetic way, and then revisited multiple times, presented and nuanced in various ways. Therefore, it is essential to keep the entirety of the work in mind in order to understand its individual parts and concepts. Certain passages become clearer in light of other analogous passages found in the text. In this way, Goodman compels the reader to adopt a "contextual" approach, in line with the clinical method he himself proposed. Thus, *Gestalt Therapy* is understood through *Gestalt Therapy* itself, by reading and re-reading. This is what I tried to do, not allowing myself to be discouraged by the difficulties of understanding I continually encountered, but rather feeling increasingly stimulated and engaged.

The writings I present here are the result of my theoretical and clinical research journey, which, I believe, I could not have reached so clearly and, I hope, meaningfully without the support of the teaching group at the Gestalt HCC Italy Institute, directed by Margherita Spagnuolo Lobb, of which I have been a part for several years. The theoretical exchanges with my teaching colleagues regarding the text by Perls, Hefferline, and Goodman, the reflections based on its group reading, and the divergences that became points for better understanding have been the fertile

DOI: 10.4324/9781003726753-1

ground, rich in thought and human contact, that has nourished the writing of all my articles.

This journey began from three areas of interest: the *theory of self*, the *technique of concentration*, and *relational Gestalt orientation*. These three themes, seemingly distinct, found a single common thread in my personal research, constituted by the attempt to reconcile, based on the self theory of Perls, Hefferline, and Goodman, the individual-centered orientation based on the use of concentration with the relational and field-centered orientation.

Since the early years of my training in Gestalt therapy, I have been particularly interested in both the Gestalt concept of self and its "partial structures," as well as in concentration and the continuum of awareness. It seemed to me that the theory of self presented in the tenth chapter of *Gestalt Therapy* was, in some respects, different from the theory of self proposed by From—or, more accurately, from how it was discussed by his students (Müller, 1993; Spagnuolo Lobb, 2001, 2016; Robine, 2004), considering that From never published anything himself. I was surprised by how rarely these differences have been explicitly addressed in the literature. Furthermore, I was struck by the fact that concentration, which had been given significant importance in both *Ego, Hunger and Aggression* (Perls, 1947/1969) and *Gestalt Therapy* (Perls, Hefferline, and Goodman, 1951), was soon set aside by Gestalt therapists, who shifted their focus from the individual to the therapeutic relationship.

Increasingly over the years, the core of the theory and methodology of Gestalt therapy has become the relational process co-created by the patient and therapist. I have followed with great interest this development to which the Institute of Gestalt HCC Italy has also made a significant contribution at an international level. I have always believed, however, that a relational perspective that neglects the internal world of the person and what Wheeler (1991) describes as "organized structures of the ground" is as one-sided and misleading as an individualistic perspective that does not consider subjective experience as a function of the field and instead isolates the person from their environment.

In all of my writings I have attempted to converge the focus on the individual and the focus on the relationship. In doing so, my intention was not so much to seek an improbable epistemological integration of the various Gestalt schools, but rather to return to the roots of Gestalt therapy, to its foundational text, where the individual and relational perspectives are presented as two sides of the same coin, two inseparable aspects of the experience, understood as a unified whole. According to Perls *et al.* (1994), individual and relationship constitute a false dichotomy. Following their teachings, Wheeler (1991) states that personal and interpersonal are the poles of awareness, understood as a "unified and organized field", which we can analyze starting from either one of the poles.

The articles collected in this volume were almost all originally published in the Institute's journal, *Quaderni di Gestalt*, over a period ranging from 2011 to 2022. In addition to the previously published works, I have added two unpublished ones: "Subjective Experience in Gestalt Therapy: Aspects and Relational

Dynamics" and "Personality, Neurotic Mechanisms, and Gestalt Diagnosis." The order of the chapters follows only partly the articles' publishing history, in order to favor some kind of thematic consistency.

In preparing this book, I used artificial intelligence tools (in particular ChatGPT-5) solely as an editorial aid to clarify, rephrase, or organize theoretical ideas that had already been developed during the course of my research. I also employed AI for the complete translation of the volume from Italian into English. The use of these tools was carried out in an ethically responsible manner and under my full supervision.

Before introducing the contents of this book, I wish to clarify that the term "phenomenology" is used here in a clinical-Gestalt sense, to describe the ways in which the self manifests in immediate experience and in the process of contact, rather than as a direct reference to the philosophical tradition. Authors such as Husserl, Heidegger, and Merleau-Ponty nevertheless remain in the background, as part of the cultural context that made the development of this perspective possible.

The first chapter offers a comprehensive analysis of the concept of subjective experience in Gestalt therapy, highlighting its evolution toward a relational perspective. It thoroughly examines the phenomenological and relational approach of Gestalt therapy, with particular emphasis on the centrality of the present moment, awareness, and the interaction between patient and therapist.

The second chapter covers the theory of the self, as presented in *Gestalt Therapy*. I present in detail the theory of the self, developed by Goodman based on the ideas of Perls, and highlight the differences between this and the interpretation provided by Isadore From, according to what the latter's students have reported.

The third chapter focuses on the Gestalt concept of spontaneity. In this chapter, I demonstrate how the therapist's spontaneity, which is never divorced from the responsibility inherent in the caregiving role, becomes a fundamental tool in therapy.

In the fourth chapter, I describe deliberate and spontaneous therapeutic activities, emphasizing how they are integrated and cannot be considered in isolation.

Chapters 5 and 6 delve into the concept of the id in Gestalt therapy. Chapter 5 explores its meaning, distinguishing it from the psychoanalytic conception: the id is not a container of unconscious drives but a mode of self-functioning that emerges in states of relaxation and non-integration. The chapter examines the role of the id in therapeutic contact, its function in the patient–therapist relationship, and its connection to field knowledge. Additionally, it explores the relationship between the id, meditation, and the spiritual dimension, highlighting how this perspective can enrich Gestalt clinical work.

The following chapter presents the Gestalt approach to dreams, based on the continuum of awareness and the functioning of the id. Unlike psychoanalytic interpretations, the proposed method emphasizes direct experience, using concentration to facilitate the integration of dream experiences. Through a clinical example, the chapter illustrates how the dream, by activating the id, can become a tool for transformation in the therapeutic process.

Chapter 6 outlines the concept of personality, emphasizing its dynamic nature and its connection to the contact process. It examines the role of character as the neurotic aspect of personality and, after describing the so-called "contact interruptions" according to the original model, presents the revisions proposed by Wheeler (1991, 2016) and Spagnuolo Lobb (2013, 2016, 2018), which, despite differences, share significant similarities. Finally, the implications of their theoretical innovations for Gestalt diagnosis are explored.

In the eighth and final chapter, I propose a systematization of the field concept, describing its various interpretations and its evolution in Gestalt literature. I then analyze certain aspects and implications through three paradigmatic categories: holism, ecology, and quantum mechanics. This approach highlights the richness and relevance of the field concept in Gestalt therapy, situating it within a historical and cultural perspective.

References

From, I., & Miller, M. V. (1994). Introduction to the Gestalt journal edition of Gestalt therapy. In F. Perls, R. Hefferline, & P. Goodman, *Gestalt therapy: Excitement and growth in the human personality* (pp. vii–xxii). Highland, NY: The Gestalt Journal Press. (Original work published 1951).

Müller, B. (1993). Isadore From's contribution to the theory and practice of Gestalt therapy. *Studies in Gestalt Therapy*, 2, 7–21.

Perls, F. (1969). *Ego, hunger, and aggression: The beginning of Gestalt therapy*. New York: Vintage Books (Random House). (Original work published 1947).

Perls, F., Hefferline, R., & Goodman, P. (1994). *Gestalt therapy: Excitement and growth in the human personality*. Highland, NY: The Gestalt Journal Press. (Original work published 1951).

Robine, J.-M. (2004). *Plis et Déplis du Self*. Bordeaux: Institut Français de Gestalt-thérapie. (Original work published 1977).

Spagnuolo Lobb, M. (2001). La teoria del sé in psicoterapia della Gestalt. In M. Spagnuolo Lobb (Ed.), *Psicoterapia della Gestalt: Ermeneutica e clinica* (pp. 86–110). Milano: FrancoAngeli.

Spagnuolo Lobb, M. (2013). *The now-for-next in psychotherapy: Gestalt therapy recounted in post-modern society*. Milano: FrancoAngeli. (Original work published 2011 as *Il now-for-next in psicoterapia*, Milano: FrancoAngeli).

Spagnuolo Lobb, M. (2016). Self as contact, contact as self: A contribution to ground experience in Gestalt therapy theory of self. In J.-M. Robine (Ed.), *Self: A polyphony of contemporary Gestalt therapists* (pp. 261–289). St. Romain de Virvèe: L'Exprimerie. (Original work published 2015 in French).

Spagnuolo Lobb, M. (2018). Aesthetic relational knowledge of the field: A revised concept of awareness in Gestalt therapy and contemporary psychiatry. *Gestalt Review*, 22(1), 50–68.

Wheeler, G. (1991). *Gestalt reconsidered: A new approach to contact and resistance*. New York, NY: Gardner Press.

Wheeler, G. (2016). The future of the self: Reflections on contact, development, and the "sub-systems of the self" in Paul Goodman. *Gestalt Review*, 20(3), 235–256.

Chapter 1

Subjective Experience in Gestalt Therapy

Aspects and Relational Dynamics

The concept of *subjective experience* represents one of the most controversial and, at the same time, one of the most fruitful theoretical and epistemological cores in the entire history of modern psychology. Although it constitutes the foundational element of human existence, its scientific legitimacy has often been questioned in favor of naturalistic and objectifying models. In this context, Gestalt therapy has had the merit of valuing lived experience from its very origins, placing it at the center of its theoretical reflection and clinical practice.

This chapter aims to explore the meaning and evolution of the concept of subjective experience in Gestalt therapy, delving into fundamental aspects such as awareness, the present moment, the surface of experience, creative self-regulation, and the holistic nature of personal lived experience. Key concepts of the Gestalt theoretical and clinical model will be presented, with particular attention to *contact*, *contact-boundary*, and *field*, which place subjective experience within a relational and co-creative framework.

1.1 Subjective Experience and Its Evolution in Modern Psychology

Subjective experience is what we live as our inner reality; it is our conscious awareness. Its contents include sensations, images, emotions, thoughts, desires, intentions, motivations, and so on, which we experience in a subjective, personal way.

Although this dimension is a central aspect of human existence, its place within modern psychology has been the subject of controversy. Emerging at the end of the 19th century, psychology adhered to the scientific model of the natural sciences, particularly physics. This paradoxically led to the exclusion of subjective experience and consciousness from psychology, as they do not conform to those criteria of scientificity. As a result, the development of modern psychology was marked by the opposition between two epistemological orientations: on one side, those who sought to adhere to the scientific-naturalistic paradigm, and on the other, those who sought to do justice to the complexity of the individual and the concrete reality of everyday life.

DOI: 10.4324/9781003726753-2

For classical behaviorism, with Burrhus F. Skinner as its most prominent exponent, psychological investigation had to completely disregard subjective experience and consciousness, focusing solely on observable behavior, understood as a mere physical event.

With the advent of the so-called "cognitive revolution," there was an apparent reevaluation of the mind in experimental psychology. However, as Morris Eagle (2024) observes, the exclusion of subjective experience remained a constant even in contemporary cognitivism. Although the latter considers cognitive and computational processes and structures as objects of study, these processes cannot be authentically defined as "mental," as they are intrinsically inaccessible to consciousness. Furthermore, cognitive psychology tends to devalue the role of consciousness, believing that individuals are little or not at all aware of the reasons and motivations underlying their behaviors.

This view of the marginal role of consciousness partially recalls classical psychoanalysis, according to which conscious subjective experience represents only the manifest content that hides and disguises the true underlying unconscious emotional meanings. In other words, conscious contents are considered unreliable, while the "true" subjective contents are concealed in the unconscious. Psychoanalysis, therefore, emphasizes the importance of the unconscious at the expense of conscious subjective experience.

Among the psychological orientations that, in contrast to naturalistic and physicalistic tendencies, have recognized the importance of subjective experience and placed it at the center of their investigation are functionalism, phenomenological-existential psychology, and humanistic psychology. These approaches recognize the complexity and centrality of lived experience. Gestalt therapy also follows this line, focusing on the experience lived by the person in the *here and now*, considering it as a phenomenological whole.

Today, the model of scientificity has evolved, after quantum physics demonstrated that there is no reality independent of the observer. This has undermined the concept of "objectivity" within the naturalistic paradigm. In fact, the very concept of what is physical remains shrouded in mystery. Nevertheless, in some fields, psychology has remained tied to a physicalistic worldview and a naturalistic model of scientificity.

1.2 Subjective Experience in Gestalt Therapy

Gestalt therapy is a phenomenological approach that explores subjective experience in the present moment, as it manifests in the individual's consciousness in the *here and now*. Every experience, in this context, is viewed as a resource for personal growth and transformation through the relationship with the external world. Subjective experience, understood in this way, becomes the primary object of investigation in Gestalt therapy.

This approach places particular emphasis on awareness of sensations and emotions. Typical questions from a Gestalt therapist might include: "How do you feel?

What are you experiencing right now? What sensations do you notice in your body as you tell me this?" For many years, individual subjective experience was the main focus of Gestalt therapy. Over time, the focus has gradually shifted from individual-centered experience to the experience of the relationship in the *here and now*.

To understand how Gestalt therapy relates to subjective experience, we can consider it through five main aspects: experience as awareness, experience of the present moment, surface experience, healthy experience, and experience as a whole. These aspects are only seemingly distinct, as each of them reflects in the others.

1.2.1 Experience as Awareness

A central concept in Gestalt therapy is *awareness*. In this context, awareness does not refer to a simple intellectual understanding or cognitive insight. Rather, it represents a state of fullness of experience, in which the individual is fully present to themselves and to the world around them. Perls, Hefferline, and Goodman (1994) state that their goal is "to shift the concern of psychiatry from the fetish of the unknown, from the adoration of the 'unconscious', to the problems and phenomenology of awareness" (p. xxv). By overcoming the traditional psychoanalytic division between conscious and unconscious, Gestalt therapy proposes a model that views experience as a unitary and continuous process of awareness.

In the Gestalt view, the unconscious is not a separate and inaccessible area of the psyche but rather a backdrop to awareness, ready to emerge when needed in response to the demands for contact with the environment. The continuous movement between figure (what is at the center of attention) and ground (what is momentarily out of awareness but can emerge) constitutes the way in which the individual experiences the world.

In the model of Perls, Hefferline, and Goodman, awareness and consciousness are distinct concepts. Awareness is immediate and spontaneous, a direct and fluid experience, while consciousness is a reflective process that activates when there is a block or difficulty in the experience. For example, I am aware when, while walking in a park, I perceive nature and enjoy the sound of birds without thinking about every step I take. In that moment, I am fully present to the experience and feel in harmony with the environment, spontaneously and immediately perceiving both my internal sensations and external stimuli. If I suddenly hear a noise behind me, consciousness comes into play: my perceptual system selectively focuses on that sound, while I wonder what it is and whether it may represent a danger. At that moment, my attention deliberately focuses, temporarily interrupting the natural flow of awareness in order to respond to the new situation. While awareness represents a state of total openness and fusion with the surrounding world, consciousness involves selection and distance from immediate experience.

Bloom (2013) observes that in the model of Perls, Hefferline, and Goodman, consciousness plays a secondary role, as it is seen as a functional interruption of awareness, aimed at solving an adaptation problem. However, according to

Bloom, human beings are rational creatures, and awareness alone cannot fully explain the complexity of human experience. Awareness and consciousness, immediate experience and reflection on experience, in his view, cannot be separated, as they continuously integrate. Consciousness is a constitutive aspect of the contact process. Bloom therefore proposes defining the continuous and dynamic flow of experience not as a *continuum of awareness*, but as a *continuum of awareness-consciousness*.

I believe that the founders of Gestalt therapy placed greater emphasis on awareness than on consciousness because they considered the development of awareness—i.e., the ability to be fully immersed in the experience of the present moment—more effective for therapeutic change than mere intellectual understanding. While the search for meaning is also an important aspect of the therapeutic process, cognitive restructuring, to be effective, must involve the patient's emotionality and constitute, according to Perls, Hefferline, and Goodman, a unitary functioning, a good contact.

Awareness is viewed by the founders of Gestalt therapy as a fundamental aspect for therapeutic change. The goal of Gestalt therapy is to guide the patient toward greater self-awareness, allowing them to be fully immersed in the flow of their immediate experiences. This process involves recognizing and integrating emotions, thoughts, physical sensations, and perceptions in the present. When a person is fully aware of these aspects in the *here and now*, they are able to recognize more clearly their own needs, desires, and blocks. This increase in awareness fosters deep transformation, leading to emotional and behavioral change.

As Bloom rightly points out, awareness and consciousness—i.e., immediate experience and reflection on that experience—are both necessary. However, it is evident that the founders of Gestalt therapy placed greater emphasis on the former, probably because it represented an unexplored territory at the time, overlooked by psychoanalysis, which focused more on the unconscious and the analysis of its contents.

The centrality of awareness in the work of Perls, Hefferline, and Goodman—who do not deny the importance of consciousness but assign it a secondary and functional role—highlights lived experience as a unitary process, emphasizing the dynamic relationship between the individual and the environment. Bloom's observations enrich this framework, creating a bridge between immediacy and reflection, between feeling and thinking, and highlighting how both dimensions are essential for understanding the complexity of human experience.

1.2.2 The Present Experience

Gestalt therapy places central importance on the experience of the present moment, which is the crucial moment in which experience occurs. Only in the *here and now* is it possible to observe, understand, and modify subjective experience.

Gestalt work can focus on the individual subjective experience of the patient or on the relationship between the patient and the therapist. On an individual level, rather than concentrating on past events or future projections, Gestalt therapy focuses on what the patient feels, thinks, and lives in the current moment, with the goal, as mentioned in the previous paragraph, of developing their awareness and fostering greater integration of their experience. On a relational level, in the present encounter, we can more effectively grasp and modify the patient's habitual relational patterns than we can through their narrative.

The past should not be ignored, but it becomes clinically relevant only to the extent that it is connected to present reality as an expression of a current need. Perls *et al.* (1994) write:

> That the present is an outgrowth of the past no-one will deny, but it does not, for instance, solve present problems to blame one's parents for the way they brought one up. Suppose, as an example, that you treasure memories of how your father has frustrated you. Such memories are important for you in actuality only insofar as you *now* feel that what you expected from your father is *still* to be fulfilled or that your resentment at its nonfulfillment is *still* to be expressed—in short, that your relationship with your father is still *presents* a problem to be attended to and solved
>
> (p. 287)

The wounds of the past manifest in the present, as they express an intentionality, a "tendency toward," a desire to reach and be reached by the other. Therapeutic change does not occur by correcting the past, but by fulfilling relational intentionality in the present. This means that therapy focuses on how the patient can fully experience the encounter with the therapist.

Work on what happens between the patient and the therapist in the present moment becomes, from a Gestalt perspective, the preferred therapeutic tool. If a patient has had relational difficulties with their father, the therapist will focus on how these difficulties reappear in the relationship between the therapist and the patient. The therapist might then ask: "How is this patient not fully experiencing the reality of our encounter here and now? What is he or she unable to express? What is he or she unable to take from the relationship with me? How might I, consciously or unconsciously, replicate the behaviors of the father?"

The past is not merely recalled but understood and processed in the *here and now* through present interaction. The goal of therapy is not so much to heal past wounds, but to modify the modes of interaction in the present. This change, in turn, may have positive effects on past wounds as well.

In summary, Gestalt therapy prioritizes immediate experience and awareness in the present moment as fundamental tools for growth and change. The interaction between the patient and the therapist in the *here and now* becomes the ground where relational and psychological blocks can be recognized and transformed. The Gestalt approach does not focus on the past as something to correct, but on the realization of an authentic and conscious encounter, with the aim of promoting a change that will also reflect on past dynamics.

1.2.3 *The Surface Experience*

As we have seen, the Gestalt therapist focuses their attention on the current experience as it is subjectively lived and as it manifests. Particular attention is therefore given to what appears on the surface. In Gestalt therapy, the term *surface* refers to all aspects of experience that are immediately perceivable and observable. These may include behaviors, emotional expressions, body language, physical sensations, and even the patient's thoughts and words, expressed without necessarily delving deeper.

Perls, Hefferline, and Goodman (1994) write: "Instead of pulling means out of the unconscious we work on the uppermost surface" (p. xxviii). While the goal of psychoanalysis is to analyze the depths of human experience, Gestalt therapy instead focuses on the surface, that is, on what is immediately accessible to the patient's awareness and the therapist's observation. Perls, Hefferline, and Goodman describe the *surface* as something *obvious*, which may seem trivial, commonplace, or insignificant. Although generally neglected, it represents the first manifestation of experience, often revealing an important gateway to explore deeper dynamics.

For example, a patient might seem to minimize their frustration over a small daily incident, such as missing the train or forgetting an appointment. However, upon observing their reaction more closely, the therapist might notice physical signs, such as tension or irritation, that indicate a deeper emotional response related to themes like self-criticism or fear of failure. In this case, the *surface* of everyday frustration becomes a pathway to explore deeper emotions and dynamics that influence the patient's behavior.

Another example of this approach could be the following:

Therapist (T): What are you feeling right now?
Patient (P): I don't know, I don't feel much.
T: You crossed your arms.
P: I didn't notice. I think it's something I do often.
T: Could you do it again, please?
P: (crosses arms again)
T: Now, try doing it a bit more intensely.
P: (crosses arms more tightly, stiffens)
T: What do you feel like this?
P: It feels like I want to say, "I don't want to talk about this."

In this case, the seemingly insignificant gesture of crossing the arms becomes an entry point to explore deeper emotions and dynamics, such as the desire to avoid a topic or a feeling of protection. Observing these surface behaviors allows the therapist to guide the patient toward greater awareness of their emotional and relational responses.

Gestalt work is not limited to observing what emerges on the surface, but also seeks to explore how the experience manifests in the present, focusing on *how* the patient lives, perceives, and expresses their experience in the *here and now*. In Gestalt therapy, the focus is not so much on *what* is happening (the content of the experience) or *why* (the explanation of the experience), but on how this experience is lived in the moment, in the *here and now*. In this way, the therapist is able to grasp dynamics that may escape purely cognitive or interpretive analysis.

This perspective also applies to dreamwork, where the focus is not on the symbolic content, but on the experiential process that emerges in the *here and now*. Attention is directed at the experience the patient lives when recounting the dream, at what they feel while telling it to the therapist. In this perspective, the dream is not interpreted but directly experienced, allowing the patient to connect with the emotions and sensations that emerge in the present moment.

In summary, focusing on what appears on the *surface* and on *how* the experience unfolds are two complementary and interconnected aspects: the *surface* provides an immediate and observable manifestation of the experience, while the *how* explores the manner in which the experience is lived, facilitating the understanding and transformation of that same experience. By working on the *surface* and the *how* of the experience, Gestalt therapy helps the patient become aware of what they are living. It also invites them to become the protagonist of their own experience, capable of fully living it, transforming it, and integrating it through direct and immediate contact with themselves and with others.

1.2.4 The Healthy Experience

Gestalt therapy does not focus on the study of neurotic experience but rather on healthy experience. When not inhibited by neurosis, experience becomes a spontaneous, creative, and self-regulating process.

From a Gestalt perspective, spontaneity is a fundamental quality for psychological well-being. It manifests when a person is fully aware of themselves and their environment, responding to present circumstances in an immediate and natural way, without being hindered by rigid patterns, *resistances*, or unintegrated past experiences. A spontaneous person faces difficulties with flexibility, adapting their behavior to the needs of the moment.

Another intrinsic quality of healthy experience is creativity, which is not limited to artistic or intellectual expression but encompasses all forms of human experience. It manifests when the individual responds to situations in an original and adaptive way, finding new and effective solutions to emerging problems.

Spontaneity and creativity are expressions of a deeper capability of the organism: psychological self-regulation, which Perls, Hefferline, and Goodman define as the *wisdom of the body*. A distinctive feature of Gestalt therapy is trust in the innate capacity of human beings to self-regulate, naturally responding to their needs through functional contact with the environment.

An example of self-regulation could be a patient who, sensing the approach of the end of the therapeutic process, begins to feel a desire for greater independence and a reduction in external support. Consciously, the patient realizes that they feel ready and, without avoiding or suppressing this need, expresses to the therapist the desire to gradually reduce the frequency of sessions. By asking to space out the appointments, the patient is acknowledging and respecting their need for autonomy, allowing the process of growth and change to continue naturally. This act reflects a spontaneous response to their psychological needs, fostering a healthy adjustment to the conclusion of the therapeutic process.

Health is closely tied to the organism's ability to self-regulate, not only physiologically, maintaining a balance of vital processes, but also psychologically, adapting flexibly and appropriately to environmental challenges and stimuli.

Psychological self-regulation enables individuals to recognize their needs and seek resources in the environment to meet them. It involves the ability to perceive the dominant need of the present moment and organize behavior to fulfill it without neurotic interference or conditioning.

It is said that a famous Zen master was asked to define Zen, and he simply replied: "When you are hungry, eat; when you are tired, sleep." This anecdote, seemingly simple and trivial, effectively illustrates the concept of spontaneous self-regulation in Gestalt therapy, emphasizing the importance of responding to present needs without interference, allowing the experience to flow freely.

Gestalt therapy recognizes in the individual an innate capacity for self-regulation, expressed through spontaneity, creativity, and a deep connection with the body. The therapeutic goal is to facilitate this natural process, enabling individuals to free themselves from blocks and interferences, so they can live a more authentic life in harmony with themselves and their surroundings.

1.2.5 The Experience as Wholeness

Subjective experience is a holistic process, an indivisible totality that, if divided, loses its Gestalt. Only from an external point of view, observing the experience in the third person, can we distinguish sensations, perceptions, emotions, thoughts, and actions. However, from the subjective point of view, the experience remains a unified whole.

Surpassing the mind-body duality, Gestalt therapy considers the emotional, cognitive, and bodily dimensions as interconnected and inseparable aspects of the self's functioning. Separating them would mean ignoring their natural interconnection. A central element of this approach is bodily awareness: the body is not considered an entity separate from the mind, but a unified and interconnected system that reflects and influences psychological experience. In therapy, the body becomes an essential tool for recognizing authentic needs and responding to life's challenges more functionally, experiencing greater integration between mind and body.

Bodily awareness is not an end in itself; it must be translated into action, allowing the person to meet their needs, strengthen their sense of self, and build self-esteem through interaction with the environment. In Gestalt therapy, action takes on a central role, as it not only meets needs but also strengthens the sense of personal efficacy and contributes to a more secure and stable identity. It is through action that our identity is revealed, and we become aware of our value. As Perls, Hefferline, and Goodman write (1994, p. 68), "the feeling of worthiness is given only by one's adequacy in an activity that is going on or in the relaxation after a completed situation."

Self-esteem does not come from abstract reflections or external judgments, but from concrete activities that allow a person to feel effective and capable of acting appropriately. It is precisely through action and its completion that the individual finds confirmation of their worth and integrates the experience into their self. As the authors of *Gestalt Therapy* emphasize, "whatever is acted has, in so far, been assimilated" (Perls, Hefferline, and Goodman, 1994, p. 203). This means that action not only meets immediate needs but also leaves a lasting imprint on personality, as every actively lived experience becomes an integral part of one's identity.

In Gestalt, direct experience is fundamental to personal growth. It is not enough to think or reflect on something: it is necessary to live it and translate it into action so that it becomes meaningful and transformative. In therapeutic practice, experiential techniques and bodily practices help patients develop awareness, address unfinished situations, and open themselves to change.

The Gestalt approach is based on a philosophy that values the integration of body, mind, and action. This holistic vision, which respects the complexity of human experience, represents a powerful engine for transformation.

1.3 Contact

Contact is a technical term that refers to the experience we have of the world in the present moment. Gestalt therapy considers subjective experience not as an isolated phenomenon, but as a relational process, co-created by the organism and the environment. Every experience involves a reciprocal interaction between organism and environment, and it is precisely this interaction that we define as *contact*. A fully lived and conscious experience is always an act of contact: a real encounter between self and world. We are inextricably linked to the environment that surrounds us.

Contact also involves the sensory and motor dimension of experience: it is a corporeal process, which always includes both sensing and acting. As Perls, Hefferline, and Goodman write (1994, p. 151): "*Contact is touch touching something.*" To live an event directly means to experience it through one's senses. In fact, contact always requires the involvement of the sensory and/or motor system—a lived and embodied participation in the experience, even if not always outwardly visible. Only when the body is involved can the experience truly be alive and transformative. Consequently, the mere acquisition of knowledge or conceptual understanding, however useful, does not constitute contact.

Contact is a creative process because it involves both assimilation and growth. The organism grows through contact with the environment, assimilating the novelty that satisfies its needs and discarding what is irrelevant or harmful. The environment continuously presents novelties that can satisfy the organism's needs, be irrelevant, or be harmful. The act of accepting useful novelty is called *identification*, while rejecting harmful novelty is referred to as *alienation*.

Experience is inherently dynamic, a process in constant motion that manifests through a continuous succession of *contacts*. Perls, Hefferline, and Goodman describe contact in terms of perceptual dynamics, through the figure/ground relationship: "Contact [...] is the forming of a figure of interest against a ground or context of the organism/environment field" (1994, p. 7). A contact is effective when the figure emerges clearly against a ground free of interference, allowing for optimal interaction between the organism and the environment. In each individual contact, a predominant need, desire, or interest emerges as the *figure*, becoming the focus of attention, while the rest—the less relevant aspects of the organism and the surrounding environment—remains in the *ground*. Once the figure is fully experienced and satisfied, it is assimilated and integrated into the ground, allowing a new figure to emerge. This continuous cycle of figure and ground allows the organism to adapt to environmental changes and grow, as each new figure offers the opportunity to evolve, satisfy new needs, and integrate new experiences.

The process of figure/ground formation is a unified process, which Perls, Hefferline, and Goodman conveniently divide into four main phases: pre-contact (perceiving a need), contact (approaching and manipulating what can satisfy it), final contact (fully experiencing the contact with what satisfies the need), and post-contact (assimilating the experience). In other words, each experience can be divided into four phases: beginning, development, critical phase, and conclusion. In any of these phases, an interruption of the process can occur, leading to a reduced capacity to feel, express oneself, and make contact. When such an interruption becomes habitual, it turns into chronic inhibition or a blockage of experience, which represents pathology. The goal of Gestalt therapy is to restore the fullness and spontaneity of experience, that is, the fluidity of the figure/ground formation process and the transition from one figure to another.

The result of contact is creative adjustment, a process that concurrently promotes the growth of the organism and the transformation of the environment. Through contact, the individual responds to their needs in an original and flexible way, adapting to circumstances and, at the same time, contributing to shaping their life context.

1.4 Contact-Boundary

Perls, Hefferline, and Goodman (1994) state that experience occurs at the *contact-boundary*, the point of meeting and exchange between the organism and the environment. When two people meet, something happens between them, not in one or the other. Each has their own subjective experience, but it is generated in the relationship, at the contact-boundary. The individual experience is always co-created in this boundary space, which is not a physical place but a metaphorical space where psychological processes unfold. The skin is an example of this boundary, which both separates and connects at the same time.

With the concept of the *contact-boundary*, Perls, Hefferline, and Goodman aim to overcome the dualistic view that separates the inner world from the outer world, the intrapsychic from the interpersonal, the individual from the relational. Psychological processes do not occur inside the individual, in the mind, nor outside of it. They are not intrapsychic or interpersonal; they are boundary events. This third dimension, a space of exchange, constitutes the specific domain of psychology.

In the context of Gestalt therapy, the *contact-boundary* fully expresses its transformative potential in the therapeutic relationship. It is not just a "place" where the patient's subjective experience is manifested, but an active and fundamental tool in the psychotherapeutic transformation process. The therapeutic relationship becomes a dynamic and reciprocal field where therapist and patient co-create an experience that promotes change and the integration of lived experience.

1.5 The Field

Another central concept in Gestalt therapy is that of "field," which Perls, Hefferline, and Goodman use to explain how the organism and the environment form a unity. The authors write in a famous passage from *Gestalt Therapy*:

> There is no single function of any animal that completes itself without objects and environment, whether one thinks of vegetative functions like nourishment and sexuality, or perceptual functions, or motor functions, or feeling, or reasoning. [...] Let us call this interacting of organism and environment in any function the "organism/environment field"; and let us remember that no matter how we theorize about impulses, drives, etc., it is always to such an interacting field that we are referring, and not to an isolated animal (Perls *et al.*, 1994, p. 4).

The organism is not an autonomous and separate entity; it can only exist in a process of continuous interconnection with the environment. The field is generated by this interconnection, and it is nothing other than this interconnection.

The Gestalt therapist observes the functioning of the field, not the functioning of the isolated organism. Every psychological event must always be considered within the organism/environment field, of which it is an expression. This means that the Gestalt therapist knows they cannot distance themselves from the patient's current experience, as they contribute to its creation moment by moment.

If the concept of the contact-boundary tells us that experience is located not inside the individual, but in the boundary space between the individual and their environment, the concept of the field indicates that the autonomy of the individual is illusory, as they are always in a relationship of interdependence with their environment.

1.6 The Evolution of the Contact Concept in Gestalt Therapy

The concept of contact in Gestalt therapy has undergone significant evolution. While the original model by Perls, Hefferline, and Goodman focused on contact as the interaction between the organism and the environment, emphasizing individual subjective experience in the present moment, the contemporary perspective has progressively shifted toward a more relational understanding. Current Gestalt therapists place at the center of their practice the reciprocal interaction in the *here and now* between patient and therapist, recognizing the relationship as a crucial element.

The original model, although conceptualizing contact as interaction, tended to focus less on the reciprocity of the exchange and to overlook the temporal dimension intrinsic to the therapeutic relationship, constituted by the series of interactions that develop over time between the two participants. Therefore, to adequately explore the complexity of the therapeutic relationship, an expansion of Gestalt's epistemological approach became necessary, fully integrating the dynamics of reciprocity and the temporal dimension of interactions.

Numerous Gestalt authors have significantly enriched the debate on the relational dimension of the therapeutic process. Among them, Wheeler (1991) and Spagnuolo Lobb (2013), as highlighted in another of my works (Macaluso, 2015), have redefined contact as an intrinsically dynamic and reciprocal process, providing a solid theoretical foundation for a relational Gestalt approach. In parallel, Hycner and Jacobs (1995) have delved into the role of the therapist as an active co-creator of the therapeutic relationship, emphasizing the crucial importance of reciprocal awareness in the present moment. Yontef and Jacobs (2009) have redefined contact as an intrinsically dynamic and reciprocal process, significantly contributing to the development of a relationally centered Gestalt approach. The collective of these and other contributions has led to a fundamental expansion of Gestalt therapy's epistemological approach, shifting attention towards an understanding of contact as an intersubjective phenomenon and enhancing the participatory role of the therapist in constructing the therapeutic relationship.

1.7 Conclusions

In this chapter, we explored the concept of subjective experience in Gestalt therapy, highlighting its central role both theoretically and clinically. Subjective experience is not viewed as an isolated mental event, but as a dynamic and relational process that manifests in the *here and now*, at the boundary between organism and environment. We discussed how Gestalt therapy focuses on present lived experience, awareness, and the importance of contact—principles that will form the foundation for the following chapters. In an era marked by the risk of fragmentation of experience and relational alienation, this approach offers a deeply humanistic clinical model capable of integrating body, emotions, thought, and action.

In the following chapters, we will delve deeper into how subjective experience unfolds in the different modes of contact and awareness, that is, in the phenomenology of the self, and how these integrate within the therapeutic context, with particular attention to the relationship and the active role of the therapist. Anchoring the therapeutic process to the centrality of lived experience and the quality of contact means considering it as an opportunity for growth, creativity, and mutual transformation. Contemporary Gestalt therapy establishes a balance between subjective experience and the therapeutic relationship, recognizing them as inseparable elements of change.

The therapeutic encounter is a dynamic relational field, where both participants contribute to the co-creation of meaning and change. This balance is reflected in the concepts of contact, contact-boundary, and field, where personal experience and interaction constantly intertwine. The awareness that the therapist has of their own experience, combined with attention to that of the patient, activates a dynamic of mutual influence that promotes emotional and psychological growth.

As we will see in the following chapters, the Gestalt therapist, aware of their active participation in the interpersonal field, becomes an integral part of the healing process, contributing with the quality of their presence and authentic expression to the co-creation of the therapeutic experience. The result is a transformation that involves both participants, in a continuous process of change in the *here and now*. The Gestalt approach, therefore, is not limited to exploring individual experience but fosters its integration in a relational context rich in meaning, where authenticity and spontaneity become the catalyst for greater awareness and lasting change.

References

Bloom, D. (2013). Situated ethics and the ethical world of Gestalt therapy. In G. Francesetti, M. Gecele, & J. Roubal (Eds.), *Gestalt therapy in clinical practice: From psychopathology to the aesthetics of contact* (pp. 131–146). Milano: FrancoAngeli.

Eagle, M. N. (2024). *Subjective experience: Its fate in psychology, psychoanalysis, and philosophy of mind.* London: Routledge.

Hycner, R., & Jacobs, L. (1995). *The healing relationship in Gestalt therapy: A dialogic/self psychology approach.* Highland, NY: The Gestalt Journal Press.

Macaluso, M. A. (2015). Beyond the Perls-Goodman model: From the organism/environment field to the relational field. *Gestalt Review*, 19(3), 233–250. (Original work published 2012 as Oltre il modello Perls-Goodman: Dal campo organismo-ambiente al campo relazionale. *Quaderni di Gestalt*, 25(2), 67–84. https://doi.org/10.3280/GEST2012-002005).

Perls, F., Hefferline, R., & Goodman, P. (1951/1994). *Gestalt therapy: Excitement and growth in the human personality.* Highland, NY: The Gestalt Journal Press.

Spagnuolo Lobb, M. (2013). *The now-for-next in psychotherapy: Gestalt therapy recounted in post-modern society.* Milano: FrancoAngeli. (Original work published 2011 as *Il now-for-next in psicoterapia*, Milano, Italy: FrancoAngeli).

Wheeler, G. (1991). *Gestalt reconsidered: A new approach to contact and resistance.* New York, NY: Gardner Press.

Yontef, G., & Jacobs, L. (2009). Gestalt therapy. In R. J. Corsini & D. Wedding (Eds.), *Current psychotherapies* (8th ed., pp. 319–357). Belmont, CA: Brooks/Cole, Cengage Learning.

Chapter 2

The Theory of the Self in Gestalt Therapy

Self, Ego, Id, and Personality[1]

The core of *Gestalt Therapy* (Perls *et al.*, 1994), the foundational text of Gestalt therapy, lies in the theory of the self formulated by Paul Goodman, based on the ideas of Fritz Perls[2]. Unlike psychoanalysis, which primarily focuses on pathology, Goodman develops his theory of the self starting from the healthy functioning of the organism, conceived holistically and in constant dynamic relationship with the environment. Adopting a phenomenological approach, he examines human experience as it manifests in its immediacy and concreteness, observing how it changes in relation to different situations. In the clinical context, Goodman identifies four fundamental modes of experience, understood as different ways of contacting the environment: the self, the ego, the id, and the personality.

By *self*, Goodman refers to spontaneous experience. When the self functions in this way, all its functions—perceptual, motor, and affective—are active and integrated. The spontaneous self represents a state of awareness and fullness of experience.

Mindful of the social factors influencing the organism/environment field, Goodman highlights society's fear of spontaneity, describing it as an *epidemic neurosis*. Society often views spontaneity as childish and irresponsible, and our culture tends to inhibit it, thus reinforcing this collective neurosis. Goodman notes that even psychological and psychoanalytic theories have largely overlooked the spontaneous self, focusing instead on the ego, the id, and the personality. Each of these concepts has, at different times and depending on the theoretical and methodological approach, been mistakenly considered as the totality of the self or, at least, its most significant part. However, the self cannot be reduced to the deliberate ego, the unconscious id, or the personality, understood as a structure of acquired attitudes devoid of vitality and originality.

Goodman revisits the ego, the id, and the personality from a process-oriented perspective, treating them as specific modes of partial functioning of the self, distinct from its spontaneous, integrated, and total functioning. Under certain circumstances, the self inhibits some of its functions, adopting configurations that correspond to particular modes of experience. Goodman calls these *partial structures* of the self. The ego, the id, and the personality are the primary partial structures of the self. The ego represents the deliberate functioning of the self,

DOI: 10.4324/9781003726753-3

characterized by will, purposeful choice, and manipulation of the environment. The id pertains to the relaxed functioning of the self, where repressed excitations resurface. The personality represents the "autonomous" functioning of the self, drawing from the reservoir of already assimilated experiences rather than responding creatively to the novelty of the environment.

Today, many Gestalt therapists refer to the theory of the self developed by Isadore From and passed down through his students (see Müller, 1993; Spagnuolo Lobb, 2001, 2013, 2016; Robine, 2004). They consider it a theoretical and practical development consistent with Goodman's model. However, there are significant differences between Goodman's theory of the self and From's, which I will attempt to outline later.[3] In this chapter, my aim is to recover Goodman's theory of the self, which has been generally neglected. To this end, I will examine the tenth chapter of the book by Perls, Hefferline, and Goodman, where the self and its primary structures are described. I will analyze each paragraph, presenting the main concepts and my interpretation of them, without claiming to provide an exhaustive analysis of the text.

2.1 Definition of the Self

In Gestalt therapy, the term *self* does not refer to a reified, stable, or continuous entity. It is neither the person nor the mind or any part of it, but rather an event, a process. Goodman defines the self as "the function of contacting the actual transient present" (Perls *et al.*, 1994, p. 149). The self is contact, the process of figure/ground formation, the making of experience in the present moment.

This process involves a constant movement between figure and ground, where every experience contributes to building and restructuring the individual's identity. Its fundamental function is creative adjustment, responding to organic needs and environmental stimuli.

The self is also described as the *system of contacts*, highlighting how various functions—such as perception, movement, and needs—work together to shape our experience. Every aspect of human experience is interconnected.

The self manifests in moments of contact, whenever an interaction occurs between the individual and the environment. Its presence can vary depending on the situation. For example, during sleep, the self is in a state of minimal activation. While the body continues to function and the mind may process dreams, active awareness and the capacity for interaction with the environment are at their lowest. Conversely, in situations requiring attention and engagement—such as performing a task or having a meaningful conversation—the self emerges more strongly and actively. The intensity of the self increases with contact and emotional involvement and diminishes during moments of confluence, where there is less distinction between organism and environment, or in states of isolation or equilibrium.

Additionally, the self is a function of the organism/environment field. "It is not the self of the organism as such, nor is it the passive recipient of the environment" (Perls *et al.*, 1994, p. 147). It is neither inside the individual nor outside them; it is neither intrapsychic nor interpersonal. The self is a boundary event, the contact-boundary at work.

Goodman defines the self, at various times, as "the system of awareness," "the power that forms the Gestalt in the field," "the agent of growth," "the integrative element," and "the maker of life." It represents the synthesis of contact processes taking place at a given moment, the continuous restructuring of the organism/environment field into meaningful wholes.

It is important to note a certain ambiguity in Goodman's definitions of the self. At times, the self is nothing more than the process of contact, while at other times, it represents the integrative element and organizing principle of that very process. Goodman deliberately acknowledges that his theory can occasionally be ambiguous and confusing, stating: "If the theory is often confusing and ambiguous, it may be that the nature too is confusing and ambiguous" (Perls *et al.*, 1994, p. 94).

2.2 The Self as the Actualization of Potential

The self expresses and actualizes itself through contact with the environment. It exists only in its realization in the present moment. Goodman defines the present moment as the transition from the past to the future. From this perspective, the present emerges as the intersection between what has been and what could be, and the self is therefore influenced by past experiences and future projections.

Our perception of time is intrinsically linked to how the self operates and evolves; it is shaped by how we live and interpret our experiences. Reality itself, far from being a fixed and immutable state, is a dynamic process constructed through contact.

In this way, Goodman succinctly and incisively presents his conception of the relationship between the self, time, and reality.

The past, consisting of *fixed forms* that are part of the background, represents a constant and essentially unchangeable state. Once events have occurred, they remain fixed in our memory and cannot be altered. However, when we focus on the current situation, what appears immutable (the past) transforms into potential, paving the way for new possibilities. Goodman emphasizes the transformative power of focused attention, which can change our perception of past experiences and generate new opportunities. This process actively reshapes experience itself.

As concentration progresses, these possibilities reorganize into a new figure that emerges from the background of potentialities. The self experiences itself and defines itself by choosing to identify with some possibilities while excluding others. This dynamic of identification and alienation is crucial, as it determines how the individual relates to the world.

The future represents the movement of this process, evolving from multiple possibilities into a single, defined figure. It is not merely a set of predetermined events but the result of the selection of current possibilities. By moving toward the new figure, the self actively contributes to shaping its own future.

Awareness of the present moment always implies a direction toward the next moment. Present experience contains, as potential, future experience. Thus, we can define the activity of the self as the realization of what is potentially inherent in the current reality.[4] In this sense, both the past and the future are implicated in the present moment.

By describing how the self develops through the process of focusing attention and selecting possibilities, Goodman provides an outline of the contact process, which he will explore in greater depth in subsequent chapters.

2.3 The Properties of the Self

Goodman identifies three fundamental properties of the self , which are deeply interconnected: spontaneity, the middle mode, and being engaged with the situation.

Spontaneity is described as a quality that arises from a deep connection with the environment. As Perls, Hefferline, and Goodman (1994) state, "Spontaneity is the feeling of acting the organism/environment that is going on, being not merely its artisan nor its artifact, but growing in it" (p. 154). In spontaneity, action is not perceived as externally imposed or as a simple reaction, but as a harmonious flow with the environment. It is neither about controlling the flow of events nor passively going along with them; rather, it involves active engagement where discovery and invention occur simultaneously[5]. In this state, action emerges naturally and fluidly, not guided solely by voluntary control or constrained by passive reactions. Goodman views spontaneity as a way of being fully immersed in the present, growing through contact with the environment.

Spontaneity represents a state of *middle mode*[6], where the individual responds creatively to situations without being entirely active or passive. This state is characterized by an attitude of *creative disinterest*, which does not imply a lack of commitment but rather openness and receptivity. It is a condition of unity that exists both before and after activity and passivity, integrating both aspects[7]. This balance allows for harmonious interaction with the environment, embracing both internal and external experiences. An example of spontaneous expression and middle mode is emotions: "One can neither will nor be compelled to feel something" (Perls *et al.*, 1994, p. 155).

The expression *engaged with the situation* refers to the way the self is perceived and experienced in relation to the present moment. When the self is absorbed in the present, it does not perceive itself as separate but experiences the situation in its entirety. In this state, the self becomes an integral part of the experience, merging with it. For example, when one is deeply immersed in an activity, one identifies with the process, and the sense of self may feel less distinct. This involvement can reach a point where the boundary between the self and the object seems to disappear. Goodman explains: "The feeling of absorption is 'self-forgetful'; it attends completely to its object" (Perls *et al.*, 1994, p. 197), and "In 'absorption' one is wholly 'in' the object" (Perls *et al.*, 1994, p. 197). A typical example is being completely absorbed in listening to music, where one becomes, as Goodman puts it, “all ears.” Goodman vividly describes this experience, in which the reflective self-awareness diminishes in full contact with the object of interest: “The figure embodies all the concern of the self, and the self is nothing but in present concern, so the self is the figure” (p. 195). Being *engaged in the situation* does not imply a total loss of the self but rather a dynamic transformation of the contact-boundary, in which the self integrates into the experience without dissolving.

As a spontaneous experience, the self integrates perceptive, motor, and affective functions into an inseparable unity. In this state, there is no separation between orientation, manipulation, and feeling. Orientation, derived from perceptions and proprioceptions, is not merely a preliminary phase but an immediate and intuitive experience, in which the individual orients themself within the action, fully living in the present moment.

In the spontaneous experience, actions are not performed based on a predefined plan or aimed at a specific goal. Orientation and manipulation occur progressively as the action unfolds, and satisfaction is derived not from achieving specific outcomes but from the process itself. This satisfaction is intrinsic to the action and evolves with it.

An effective example is that of a warrior deeply engaged in a mortal battle, experiencing a passionate and total involvement in the action. The fight is lived as a complete experience, where every moment is meaningful, and the warrior finds both pleasure and meaning in the action itself. This illustrates how, in a state of full immersion, the self manifests through spontaneous action, dynamically integrating with the environment and softening the perception of a separate self-awareness while maintaining the boundary necessary for the assimilation of the experience. The contact-boundary remains active even in states of deep immersion.

Goodman draws upon the three grammatical persons—*I*, *You*, and *It*—previously discussed in the seventh chapter as characteristics of the flow of speaking. In the tenth chapter, these evolve into three dimensions of the creative adjustment process. The *I* represents the self-awareness the organism has of itself; the *It* embodies motivational desires and needs, while the *You* is the object of interest.

When the self is engaged in the present situation, the *I* exists in a polar relationship with the *You* and the *It*, creating a functional unity. This triad helps understand how the self manifests in the spontaneous mode, highlighting how each element interacts with and influences the others in the process of creative adjustment.[8] In this engaged state, the self is not abstractly self-aware but experiences the situation through these three dimensions, integrating perceptions and emotions into a continuous flow of interaction with the environment.

2.4 The Structures of the Self

Until now, following Goodman’s exposition, we have considered the self in its optimal mode of functioning: a unified and spontaneous process, a totality of sensory, perceptual, and motor functions that manifests when we feel deeply engaged with the present situation and are fully absorbed in it. However, of course, the self does not always operate in this way, although certain particularly sensitive and gifted individuals may frequently experience moments of intense creativity. In many circumstances the self does not operate spontaneously, but structures itself in specific forms, to respond to the demands of the environment and adapt to various situations. This process occurs by blocking or fixing certain aspects of the self to allow others to activate freely.

Goodman mentions, as examples of these partial structures, both neurotic configurations—marked by rigid and repetitive patterns—and specific adaptive modes, such as the structure of naturalistic observation, in which one perceives objects with an attitude of deliberate objectivity, refraining from actively manipulating them. According to Goodman, phenomenological psychology should systematically classify, describe, and analyze these varied possible structures of the self.

Because of their clinical and theoretical importance, Goodman particularly emphasizes three fundamental partial structures of the self: the ego, the id, and the personality. He suggests that certain psychological theories and clinical approaches, influenced by the kinds of patients and techniques used, have mistakenly overlooked the integrated and spontaneous self, incorrectly viewing these partial structures as if they represented the self's total functioning.

Goodman offers an innovative interpretation of the ego, id, and personality, linking them to phases of the figure/ground formation process. He clearly distinguishes two related but separate concepts: *phases* and *structures* of the self.

Phases refer to the temporal moments of the spontaneous figure/ground process under optimal conditions. *Structures*, instead, are specific and partial configurations that the self temporarily adopts when its spontaneous integration is inhibited or limited.

In spontaneous functioning, ego, id, and personality appear as fluid and integrated phases of a unified process. When spontaneity is limited, these phases may temporarily stabilize into distinct partial structures, each characterized by a specific mode of functioning. In this way, the self dynamically adapts to particular contexts and demands.

Goodman describes these phases as follows:

The id is the first outcropping of a figure from the background, encompassing organic excitations, the initial awareness of unfinished situations from the past, vague perceptions of the environment, and the earliest sensations that connect the organism with its surroundings. At this preliminary stage, these elements are spontaneous, diffuse, and undefined, but through interaction with the environment they gradually take shape and become structured into a clear and coherent figure.

The ego manifests through a progressive identification with certain possibilities and the simultaneous alienation of others. In this phase, the individual deliberately limits and intensifies the field of contact to focus on specific aspects of the situation. Interaction with the environment is expressed through motor behavior, orientation, and manipulation, supported by aggression as the vital energy that enables actively shaping and transforming experience.[9]

The personality is the figure that the self becomes at the final stage of the contact process, assimilated into the organism and integrated with the results of previous growth. Each successful contact thus contributes to a relatively stable set of attitudes and capacities that support further development and creative interaction with the environment.

In fully spontaneous situations—where identification with impulses, objects, or actions occurs immediately and without deliberate alienation—it is neither necessary nor useful to distinguish explicitly between id, ego, and personality. However, Goodman emphasizes that this distinction becomes crucial when the self temporarily adopts partial structures, interrupting its spontaneous integration. In such cases, each dimension (id, ego, personality) appears as a distinct, temporary mode of functioning, providing valuable insight for psychological analysis and therapeutic practice. Thus, while Goodman initially describes these dimensions as developmental phases within the spontaneous process, he also reinterprets them as specific partial structures—a perspective explored in the following paragraphs.

2.5 The Ego

As we have just mentioned, in spontaneous situations, where identification with what is given is immediate, "the ego is a progressing stage of the self-function" (Perls *et al.*, 1994, p. 164). However, in healthy experiences, the situation is often different. In these cases, the individual initially finds themselves in a state of relaxation, open to multiple interests, which are accepted without immediate involvement. When one of these interests gains greater relevance, activating energy and attention, the individual can deliberately choose to focus on it, unless conflicting interests resolve themselves spontaneously.

After describing the characteristics of the self in its spontaneous form, Goodman now examines the characteristics of the ego, or more precisely, the 'self-awareness of the ego,' that is, the individual's perception of themselves in a deliberate experience. The self-awareness of the ego is "deliberate, active in mode, sensorily alert and motorically aggressive, and conscious of itself as isolated from its situation" (Perls *et al.*, 1994, p. 157).

The ego operates in an active mode, being deliberate and action-oriented: it makes conscious decisions about what to notice and what to exclude (selective attention), establishes boundaries between itself and the environment, and acts upon the environment with intentionality rather than simply being passively involved in a spontaneous way. Furthermore, it is vigilant and controls the experience rather than being immersed in it without distinction. The ego is also described as motorically aggressive, where aggression does not imply hostility but rather a proactive energy that expresses itself in interaction with the environment through action.

In the spontaneous self, the individual experiences reality in a unified manner, without a clear distinction between themselves and the world. In the deliberate ego, however, they perceive themselves as a separate agent, capable of choosing, controlling, and directing action. The perception of this distinction between oneself and the situation is essential for maintaining boundaries, making choices, and acting autonomously. Let's consider a concrete example. If a person listens to music spontaneously, they allow themselves to be carried away by the experience without perceiving a separation between themselves and the sound. If, instead, they decide to carefully analyze the structure of the music (looking for chords, rhythm, harmony), they enter an active and deliberate mode, typical of the ego.

In the transition from a spontaneous experience to a deliberate one, the ego fragments and abstracts the original unity of the experience, isolating specific parts to control them more effectively. In spontaneous experience, what one does, how one does it, and why one does it are closely connected. In deliberate experience, however, through abstraction, these elements become separate: the project is distinct from the means needed to accomplish it and from the final goal. This allows for better focus and structuring of action but, at the same time, reduces the fluidity and naturalness of the lived experience.

Goodman also highlights that when one reflects on their psychological functioning through introspection, the ego becomes the dominant structure, while the global self (that is, the self in its integrated and spontaneous functioning) is relegated to the background or undervalued. This explains why many psychological theories, based on self-analysis, tend to place excessive emphasis on the ego rather than considering the self in its totality.

Finally, Goodman highlights a neurotic mechanism that influences the perception of the self and pushes traditional psychoanalytic theories to consider the ego as the central structure of the self. In unresolved neurotic situations, deliberative acts tend to repeat themselves, leaving a deep imprint on the perception of the self. Conversely, spontaneous contacts, which naturally resolve situations, tend to be forgotten. Consequently, traditional psychoanalytic theories end up emphasizing the role of the ego, ignoring the self in its totality and its natural functioning. An example helps clarify the concept. If a person engages in a conversation without worries, they live the moment, interact, and then forget the episode. If, instead, the person has social anxiety, during the conversation, they become hyper-aware of their words and actions. After the meeting, they will continue to rethink what they said and how they behaved. This mental repetition reinforces the perception of an insecure self and accentuates the centrality of the ego in memory.

2.6 The Id

For psychoanalysis, conscious content holds little value and is considered unreliable. Consciousness plays a marginal role compared to the fundamental importance of the id, the unconscious and inaccessible dimension of the psychic apparatus.

This conception of the id stems from Freud's therapeutic method, in which the patient, in a state of relaxation and passivity, allows mental associations to flow freely. The meanings of the material produced in this state do not arise from the patient themselves but from the psychoanalyst's interpretation.

Goodman reinterprets the id from a phenomenological and process-oriented perspective: for him, the id does not represent an unconscious dimension but a mode of the self, a dimension of conscious experience. While the ego represents the active, deliberative, and highly structured mode of the self, the id is characterized by relaxation, passivity, and a state of non-integration.

Goodman illustrates the id through the example of a common state of relaxation, such as the twilight phase before sleep when the self suspends sensory attention and loosens muscular tension. In this state, the self appears passive and disorganized, dominated by imaginative and hallucinatory content. The feeling of passivity arises because the self accepts what emerges without actively intervening.[10] Images, impressions, and fleeting fantasies appear and disappear without any attempt to engage with them. The figure–ground dynamic does not develop, leaving these images transient and undeveloped into more structured experiences. In self-awareness, these impressions are perceived as something that simply happens; the individual experiences them passively, without the deliberate activation characteristic of the ego.

During this state of relaxation, unmet needs or unfinished situations from the day may resurface in the form of images or fantasies, as seen in hypnagogic visions or fantasies associated with masturbation. These images offer partial relief, temporarily satisfying needs that, if too pressing, could disrupt relaxation and lead to insomnia or restlessness.

In the absence of active interaction with the environment, the self tends to disintegrate and dissolve, reducing itself to a state of pure potentiality. The body becomes central, as repressed bodily sensations resurface into consciousness. If these sensations do not become the focal point of attention, the individual slips into sleep.

Goodman views the id as the relaxation and temporary dissolution of the self's structures—a condition in which repressed bodily sensations emerge. It represents a state of potentiality, an openness to the spontaneous formation of an emerging figure. This relaxation allows the subject to connect more directly with sensations and desires often repressed in daily life. In another passage, Goodman defines the id as a mode of "relaxation and loose association" of the self (Perls *et al.*, 1994, p. 19), simultaneously indicating a state of ease and the flow of experiences that arise from it.[11]

Thus, the Gestalt id is not static or mysterious but a mode of the self that manifests under particular conditions when defenses are lowered, and attention becomes open to spontaneous sensations, impulses, and desires. Consequently, the Gestalt therapeutic process does not rely on the interpretation of unconscious content by the therapist but is configured as a dynamic experience where the patient takes center stage. Through the id, the patient can explore the present experience in an immediate and spontaneous way.

2.7 The Personality

According to Goodman, the concept of *personality* is also shaped by the methods used in psychotherapy, particularly those aimed at analyzing and altering interpersonal relationships. Goodman defines personality as "the system of attitudes assumed in interpersonal relations" (Perls *et al.*, 1994, p. 160). Personality is not a fixed structure but rather a dynamic set of behaviors, attitudes, and ways of being that manifest within the context of social interactions. Through these experiences, individuals develop a representation of themselves that allows them to recognize who they are and communicate to others why they act in a certain way.

Personality is essentially verbal in nature: "It is useful to define 'personality' as a structure of speech habits" (Perls et al., 1994, p. 100). According to Goodman, personality is deeply rooted in the linguistic and communicative dimension. Language, in this perspective, is not merely a tool for communication but also a means through which individuals organize and attribute meaning to their experiences.

In a state of neurosis, personality is constructed based on distorted self-representations. These include erroneous conceptions, introjects (ideas or values passively assimilated from external sources), unrealistic ego ideals, and masks adopted to adapt to specific situations.

At the end of a therapeutic journey, the individual will have developed a certain level of self-awareness and achieved good adaptation. According to traditional therapeutic approaches (such as psychoanalysis), this outcome corresponds to a free and well-adapted personality capable of managing social relationships in a balanced and functional manner. However, Goodman views this as an adaptation that suppresses the individual's more spontaneous, vital, and creative aspects. He also criticizes the perspective, particularly upheld by the Washington School (Sullivan, Fromm, Horney), which tends to conflate personality with the integral self, reducing the latter to a purely social and relational construct.

After exploring the self-awareness of the ego and the id, Goodman introduces the self-awareness of personality, which refers to the individual's perception of themselves, their emotional and psychological state, as they engage with the environment based on accumulated experiences and their identity. This self-awareness is characterized by autonomy, transparency, and responsibility.

Autonomy involves actions that reflect the individual's identity, personal evolution, and values, integrating past and present experiences. When faced with something new, individuals interpret and assimilate it based on what they have already experienced. In other words, the past always influences the present.

Goodman differentiates between autonomy and spontaneity, two distinct modalities of the self through which the individual interacts with the environment.

Autonomy is the ability to make free and conscious choices based on who one is and their personal evolution. It is grounded in the security that comes from accumulated experiences and abilities. Autonomy represents a balance between the activity of deliberateness (ego) and the passivity of relaxation (id). It is neither entirely active nor wholly passive but a synthesis that involves acting consciously and consistently with one's personal development.

Spontaneity, on the other hand, does not offer the same sense of freedom or security as autonomy because it consists of an immediate and intuitive response to the present situation. In the *middle mode* of spontaneity, action occupies a position of balance between control and passivity. This should not be confused with the equilibrium of autonomy, as it involves a deep engagement with the present, where the self expands beyond its usual limits, acting in harmony with the environment.

Goodman defines personality as *transparent*, meaning observable and definable, because it represents the sum of what has been consciously recognized and what the individual can understand and describe clearly. In the therapeutic context, this transparency derives from the insights that emerge during the process of self-awareness. Unlike personality, the self is not transparent because it is not an autonomous entity. It does not perceive itself directly as such; rather, its self-awareness is situational and relational, as it emerges in the present experience and in its relationship with others.

Another characteristic of personality is the sense of responsibility, which implies the ability to be accountable for one's actions and their related consequences, acting in accordance with one's commitments and personal values. Responsibility requires consistency in behavior, whereas spontaneity does not follow a predetermined plan but develops its own coherence in the course of action. Personality, therefore, is the self's responsible structure, capable of responding to social and interpersonal demands.

2.8 Goodman's Theory of the Self and From's Theory

Generally, Gestalt therapists refer to the interpretation of the theory of the self developed by Isadore From, considering it a coherent development of Goodman's ideas. From, a prominent figure in Gestalt therapy, is known for his in-depth study and teaching of the theory of the self, although he left no written works. Our knowledge of his thought comes from oral accounts and the testimonies of his students.

Bertrand Müller, a student of From, collected his teachings and, in an article (Müller, 1993), summarized his contribution to the theory and practice of Gestalt therapy. It is this summary that I draw upon to present From's ideas. From reinterpreted and redefined the aspects of the self described by Goodman, more precisely referring to them as *functions of the self*. He describes the self as a set of three functions—the id-function, the ego-function, and the personality-function—which he considers interconnected processes through which the individual continuously regulates contact with the environment.

The id-function pertains to the organism's primary needs and impulses, essentially answering the question, "What do I need?" The ego-function enables a person to choose, act, and consciously direct their energy in response to the needs arising from the id-function, answering the question, "What do I want?" The personality-function gathers and integrates the individual's history, habits, beliefs, and sense of identity, answering the question, "Who am I?"

These functions work together to allow an individual to feel, desire, and define themselves. When the ego-function is "lost" (that is, when the person is no longer able to consciously and deliberately direct their actions), the id-function and the personality-function are also disrupted, leading to psychological distress. From identifies four ways in which the *loss of the ego-function* can occur: confluence, introjection, projection, and retroflection. According to From, the therapist's task is to restore the patient's ability to directly experience how they are altering their contact-boundary, helping them to recover the ego-function and, with it, the overall balance of the self.

From's interpretation of the theory of the self, however, appears to diverge in some respects from Goodman's original theory. As we have seen, Goodman distinguishes between a mode of total functioning of the self (spontaneity) and three modes of partial functioning of the same self (deliberateness, relaxation, and autonomy). From, on the other hand, focuses solely on three functions of the self (id-function, ego-function, and personality-function), overlooking the self as a mode of integrated and spontaneous functioning. According to Müller (1993), From primarily identified the self with the ego-function. Wheeler's testimony further confirms the centrality that From attributed to the ego. Here is how Wheeler (2016) recounts what From often repeated to him on this subject:

> Gestalt therapy is a therapy only of the "ego." Id is a given that has nothing to do with therapy. Personality is a fiction: that also has nothing to do with therapy. All Gestalt therapy can do [...] is to focus on ego, which is the "identifying with and alienating of possibilities." That is the only thing that we can change, in therapy.
> (p. 246)

It would seem, then, that From placed particular emphasis on the ego, even identifying it with the self, whereas Goodman, in *Gestalt Therapy*, focused primarily on the creative and spontaneous self, which serves as the foundation of his theoretical and clinical model.

Another point of divergence between Goodman's and From's theories of the self concerns their understanding and use of the concepts of ego, id, and personality as structures or functions of the self. According to Wheeler (2016), the partial structures of the self represent the most incoherent and least essential part of Goodman's model, which he considers 'baroque and useless appendages. Wheeler cites the testimony of Taylor Stoehr, Goodman's friend and biographer, who, regarding the partial structures of the self described in *Gestalt Therapy*, states:

> The book dragged on [...] and I think Paul just wanted to get it finished. He didn't really care that much about the theory of the self, and those sub-parts. It was the basic thing of the autonomous self in action that mattered to him, in

> Gestalt theory. You can tell that reading it. [...] I never heard him say another word about ego, or personality; id, maybe.
>
> (Wheeler, 2016, p. 248)

In my view, Goodman did not pay much attention to the partial structures of the self—not because he was rushing to complete *Gestalt Therapy*, as Stoehr suggests, but because they were genuinely a secondary aspect of his theoretical model. Goodman offers a phenomenological and process-oriented conception of the self, corresponding to the full and spontaneous unfolding of experience. It is this optimal mode of experience that he is most interested in, as Stoehr himself highlights. Goodman critiques psychoanalytic theories that, from time to time, reduce the self to the ego, the id, or the personality. He reinterprets these static and abstract concepts in processual terms, respectively as deliberateness, relaxation, and autonomy. Thus, Goodman incorporates psychoanalytic notions of ego and id into his theoretical framework to revise them through a phenomenological lens, not to make them central or defining elements of the Gestalt model.

In From's interpretation of the theory of the self, however, the ego-function, id-function, and personality-function take on particular theoretical and clinical significance, becoming distinctively Gestalt concepts (see Müller, 1993). He considers these functions as an operational framework for therapeutic work, helping to identify where and how to intervene (needs: *id-function*; will and action: *ego-function*; identity: *personality-function*).

To summarize, Goodman adopts a philosophical-existential view: the self is an event, the process of contacting the environment, with its three components describing different moments or modalities. From, on the other hand, proposes a more methodical and clinically oriented model, referring to "functions" to emphasize their operational dimension: they are not intrapsychic locations or fixed structures but functioning modes the therapist can observe and work with. At the center of Goodman's vision is spontaneity: the "total functioning of the self." From, in contrast, assigns decisive importance to the ego-function: when this is "lost," the other functions (id and personality) are "disturbed" as a result. In this sense, From identifies the loss of the ego-function as the root of all psychological suffering.

Goodman's ideas on the structures of the self stem from a critique of the rigidity of traditional psychoanalytic concepts, which he reinterprets in processual terms without making them the cornerstone of his model. From, however, adopts those same psychoanalytic categories (ego, id, personality) and transforms them into "functions of the self," giving them strong theoretical and methodological significance. These functions form the backbone of From's Gestalt theory and practice, with the ego-function at the forefront as the lever for therapeutic change.

Regarding clinical implications, Goodman emphasizes spontaneity as the ideal condition: a full experience in which the organism is fully immersed in the present moment and creatively adapts to the environment in the best possible way. From aims to restore the ego-function to enable the patient to consciously direct their actions and relationships.

At this point, a clarification is warranted. The considerations presented thus far regarding the importance From seems to have placed on the deliberate ego rather than the spontaneous self do not necessarily reflect how he worked in practice. Those who knew him closely attest to From's extraordinary clinical sensitivity. He was capable of living the here and now of the relationship so intensely and spontaneously that he resonated deeply with the other's experience, to the point of visibly trembling during his sessions. We have precise testimony of this, which I will mention in the next chapter.

However, in my view, the theory of the self as passed down from does not do justice to the centrality that spontaneity holds in Goodman's theory. I believe it is important to reclaim Goodman's vision of the self and its partial structures, understood as deliberateness, relaxation, and autonomy, given the many significant clinical implications it can offer. In the following chapters, I will attempt to illustrate some of these implications.

2.9 Conclusions

The Gestalt self represents the state of awareness and spontaneity in which a person, in creative union with the environment, responds appropriately and naturally to present situations. It acts harmoniously and effectively, without rational calculation or effort, embracing the risk of novelty with trust in one's own capabilities, unconcerned with outcomes or self-image. This vital and creative way of being can be found "in the spontaneity of children, in the works of heroes, the culture of classical eras, the community of simple folk, the feeling of lovers, the sharp awareness and miraculous skill of some people in emergencies" (Perls *et al.*, 1994, p. 97).

If *Gestalt Therapy* is considered the "Bible" by Gestalt therapists—fondly referred to as such for its foundational importance—the "good news" it proclaims is precisely the creative, integrative, and transformative power of the self.

Goodman highlights the complementary relationship between the spontaneous self and the deliberate ego, considering them as two integrated modalities of human experience. However, in neurosis, deliberateness tends to replace spontaneity rather than integrate with it. In the sixth chapter of *Gestalt Therapy*, the phylogenetic evolution of contact with the environment is described, showing how, throughout the history of the species, humans have transitioned from an immediate and intuitive sensory mode to a more reflective and rational one. While inherently healthy and advantageous, the latter becomes dysfunctional when it dominates spontaneity instead of collaborating with it.

Goodman criticizes modern society for separating the ego from the self and assigning the ego a disproportionate role. To restore balance, it is necessary to strengthen the spontaneous self, reinstating its essential function alongside deliberateness. From this perspective, psychotherapy aims to foster spontaneity, reducing neurotic deliberateness to promote a more integrated and harmonious experience.

Even in the psychotherapeutic process, there is a risk that deliberateness might overshadow spontaneity, leading the therapist to rely primarily on the deliberate resources of both themselves and the patient, rather than on their mutual spontaneous self-regulation. However, an excessively reflective, rational, and controlled therapeutic action risks being less effective.

Goodman emphasizes this point by stating:

> Especially in psychotherapy: habitual deliberateness, factuality, non-commitment, and excessive responsibility, traits of most adults, are neurotic; whereas spontaneity, imagination, earnestness and playfulness, and direct expression of feelings, traits of children, are healthy.
>
> (Perls *et al.*, 1994, p. 82)

The novelty of Gestalt therapy lies in its way of conceiving the free, vital, and spontaneous functioning of the self—an experience that emerges when one is fully immersed in the present moment and in harmony with the environment. This state represents the essence of psychological health and the core of therapeutic work, which aims to discover the individual's creative potential and deepest resources (*see Spagnuolo Lobb and Amendt-Lyon, 2003*).

The second volume of *Gestalt Therapy*, written by Hefferline, outlines a path for developing awareness through a series of gradual concentration experiments, closely resembling certain techniques from Buddhist meditation.[12]

I believe that one of the fundamental tasks for today's Gestalt therapists is to reclaim the centrality of the spontaneous self, as described in *Gestalt Therapy*, while integrating it with the growing focus on the co-created relational dimension of psychotherapy—a hallmark of our approach's evolution in recent years. I will address this theme in the next two chapters.

Notes

1 Revised version of a work previously published in *Quaderni di Gestalt*, 2015, XXVIII, 2: 61–78. DOI: 10.3280/GEST2015-002004.

2 As is well known, the theoretical portion of *Gestalt Therapy: Excitement and Growth in the Human Personality*—originally published as the second volume—was written by Paul Goodman, who developed and expanded a preliminary manuscript by Frederick Perls. Ralph Hefferline, on the other hand, contributed to the practical section of the work, drafting what would become the first volume. While it is not possible to precisely determine Goodman's specific contributions to the development of the new psychotherapy model presented in the second volume, it is evident that his role in its theoretical formalization was significant. In the remainder of this chapter, I will primarily refer to Goodman, with the understanding that his theoretical work is grounded in Perls' insights and ideas.

3 On the difference between Goodman's theory of the self and that of From, see also Philippson (2001).

4 This conception of present experience as potentiality, openness to the future, and a tension toward the next figure underpins the concept of "now-for-next," proposed by the Polsters (1974) and developed further by Spagnuolo Lobb (2013), as well as the concept of "intentionality of contact," proposed by the Istituto di Gestalt HCC (Cavaleri, 2003). Both concepts, "now-for-next" and "intentionality of contact," are based on the premise

that the present is not merely a static moment but rather a starting point for evolution and personal growth. This interconnectedness between the present, potentiality, and the future is central to Gestalt therapy and provides a dynamic and relational perspective on human experience.

5 According to Goodman, the act of "discovering-and-inventing" is intrinsic to the spontaneous self and represents the core of creative adjustment. This verb reflects the self's attitude when functioning in a state of balance between active and passive—what is referred to as the "middle mode." In this perspective, "discovering" refers to the aspect of experience where the individual perceives and recognizes new or unexpected elements in the environment, while "inventing" denotes the ability to transform and give meaning to these elements, integrating them into their lived experience.

6 The term 'middle mode,' used by Goodman, refers to the 'middle voice' of verbs in the Ancient Greek language.

7 Goodman refers to the concept of "creative indifference," which Perls borrowed from Salomo Friedlaender. For more on Friedlaender's thought and its influence on Perls, see Frambach (2003).

8 According to Adlington (1977), Buber's dialectical existentialism, which defines the intertwining relations of *I* with *Thou* and *It*, serves as a model for Goodman, in opposition to the Cartesian concept of an isolated, self-originating consciousness.

9 *Orientation* refers to the perceptual and cognitive process by which relevant elements of the organism–environment field are identified. *Manipulation* involves concrete actions aimed at transforming the environment to meet a need. Together, they represent complementary aspects of how the ego functions in the process of creative adjustment, allowing a dynamic and intentional response to the organism's needs. In this context, aggressiveness is not negatively connoted but is understood as a vital, creative force that enables decisive action, addressing and transforming reality to achieve satisfaction.

10 In this context, the passivity of the self should be understood as receptivity. Although the id is not active in the deliberative sense of the ego, it still involves a dynamic process of the emergence of experiences.

11 In the Gestalt approach, the psychoanalytic technique of free association is replaced by a similar technique that integrates psychosomatic, verbal, and cognitive elements. This technique was later defined by Perls during his Californian period as the *continuum of awareness*.

12 The first Perls (1947/1969) already believed that the development of the ability to concentrate, which is essentially a form of meditation, represented the main way to recover organic spontaneity.

References

Adlington, H. (1997). Paul Goodman: An approach to language. *Studies in Gestalt Therapy*, 6/7, 31–44.

Cavaleri, P. A. (2003). *La profondità della superficie: Percorsi introduttivi alla psicoterapia della Gestalt*. Milano: FrancoAngeli.

Frambach, L. (2003). The weighty world of nothingness: Salomo Friedlaender's "creative indifference". In M. Spagnuolo Lobb & N. Amendt-Lyon (Eds.), *Creative license: The art of Gestalt therapy* (pp. 113–127). Wien/New York, NY: Springer.

Macaluso, M. A. (2015). La teoria del sé in Gestalt Therapy: Il sé, l'Io, l'Es e la personalità. *Quaderni di Gestalt*, 28(2), 61–78. https://doi.org/10.3280/GEST2015-002004

Müller, B. (1993). Isadore from's contribution to the theory and practice of Gestalt therapy. *Studies in Gestalt Therapy*, 2, 7–21.

Perls, F. (1969). *Ego, hunger and aggression: The beginning of Gestalt therapy*. New York: Vintage Books (Random House). (Original work published 1947).

Perls, F., Hefferline, R., & Goodman, P. (1951/1994). *Gestalt therapy: Excitement and growth in the human personality*. Highland, NY: The Gestalt Journal Press.

Philippson, P. (2001). *Self in relation*. Highland, NY: The Gestalt Journal Press.

Polster, E., & Polster, M. (1974). *Gestalt therapy integrated: Contours of theory and practice*. New York, NY: Vintage Books.

Robine, J.-M. (2004). *Plis et Déplis du Self*. Bordeaux: Institut Français de Gestalt-thérapie. (Original work published 1977).

Spagnuolo Lobb, M. (2001). La teoria del sé in psicoterapia della Gestalt. In M. Spagnuolo Lobb (Ed.), *Psicoterapia della Gestalt: Ermeneutica e clinica* (pp. 86–110). Milano: FrancoAngeli.

Spagnuolo Lobb, M. (2013). *The now-for-next in psychotherapy: Gestalt therapy recounted in post-modern society*. Milano: FrancoAngeli. (Original work published 2011 as *Il now-for-next in psicoterapia*, Milano: FrancoAngeli).

Spagnuolo Lobb, M. (2016). Self as contact, contact as self: A contribution to ground experience in Gestalt therapy theory of self. In J.-M. Robine (Ed.), *Self: A polyphony of contemporary Gestalt therapists* (pp. 261–289). St. Romain de Virvèe: L'Exprimerie. (Originally published 2015 in French).

Spagnuolo Lobb, M., & Amendt-Lyon, N. (Eds.). (2003). *Creative license: The art of Gestalt therapy*. Wien/New York, NY: Springer.

Wheeler, G. (2016). The future of the self: Reflections on contact, development, and the "sub-systems of the self" in Paul Goodman. *Gestalt Review*, 20(3), 235–256.

Chapter 3

The Spontaneity of the Therapeutic Encounter as a Key Factor for Change[1]

The recent developments in Gestalt therapy, starting from the 1990s, have placed greater emphasis on the relational aspects of this approach, which were already present in essence in *Gestalt Therapy* (Perls *et al.*, 1994). According to Spagnuolo Lobb (2013), in the current socio-cultural context, marked by a lack of intimate relationships and the inability to contain the excitement of encountering the other, the fundamental task of psychotherapy becomes "to give tools of horizontal relational support, that can make people feel recognized by the glance of the equal other" (p. 29). From this perspective, care does not primarily consist of providing the patient with support to express their inhibited needs but rather in offering them an experience of encounter that allows them to restore the spontaneity of the self. Awareness, a central concept in Gestalt therapy that denotes being centered on the present moment, is understood in the therapeutic situation in relational terms. Spagnuolo Lobb writes (2013, p. 46):

> Being in the present is […] a being in the reality of the situation (both the patient's and the therapist's), in the reality of their human finiteness, and it is by staying in this shared finiteness that they are both directed towards the therapeutic aim. The process of contact-withdrawal from contact is experienced for itself, with a view to finding in this relationship alternative perceptions that will make possible a spontaneity of contact, a wholeness of one's being-with.

This requires the Gestalt therapist to be willing to become emotionally involved in the therapeutic relationship and to be able to respond to the other in a personal and spontaneous way. While in an individual-centered perspective the fundamental therapeutic tool is the exploration of experience through concentration, in the new relational perspective, the therapist's spontaneity becomes the key instrument. Today, the Gestalt therapist is called upon to foster the patient's spontaneity through their own ability to be spontaneous and authentic. In their work, spontaneity constitutes both the means and the end at the same time.

In this perspective, the concept of spontaneity takes on a central role. Spagnuolo Lobb, in line with the teachings of Perls, Hefferline, and Goodman, defines it as "the quality that accompanies being fully present at the contact-boundary, with

DOI: 10.4324/9781003726753-4

full awareness of oneself and with full use of our senses" (Spagnuolo Lobb, 2013, p. 86). Understood in this way, spontaneity becomes a specific requirement for the Gestalt therapist.

In this chapter, I will attempt to address some questions related to spontaneity and its therapeutic function from a Gestalt perspective. What is spontaneity, and what are its characteristics? What is its value from a therapeutic standpoint? How is the spontaneity of being in a relationship learned? How can spontaneity be reconciled with the specific responsibilities inherent in the therapeutic role? These are complex and open-ended questions. This work aims to contribute to the ongoing reflection on these issues.

3.1 Concentration, Awareness, and Spontaneity in *Ego, Hunger and Aggression*

In his first book, *Ego, Hunger and Aggression* (1947/1969), Perls places particular emphasis on "positive concentration," which he distinguishes from what is commonly understood as concentration. In the common understanding, concentration refers to the effort of deliberately focusing attention on something. According to Perls, this type of concentration is negative and harmful, as it is tied to a sense of duty and characterized by intense muscular contractions and an effort that leads to fatigue and irritability. Positive concentration, on the other hand, consists of being totally and spontaneously focused on something that arouses our interest. In terms of figure–ground dynamics, in positive concentration, the figure is strong and relatively stable, whereas in negative concentration, the figure is made unstable by what is deliberately excluded from attention and tends to become a figure instead of remaining in the background. Here is how Perls describes positive concentration, which he considers a state of fascination:

> The object occupies the foreground without any effort, the rest of the world disappears, time and surroundings cease to exist; no internal conflict or protest against the concentration arises. Such concentration is easily found in children, and often in adults when engaged in some interesting work or hobby. As every part of the personality is temporarily coordinated and subordinated to one purpose only, it is not difficult to realize that such an attitude is the basis of every development.
>
> (Perls, 1947/1969, p. 188)

Perls also distinguishes between *self-awareness* and *self-consciousness* and illustrates the difference between these two concepts with the following example:

> When, for instance, you are so fully absorbed in dancing that you feel the oneness of mind, body, soul, music and rhythm, then you realize the pleasure of self-awareness, of the "feeling" yourself. But there might be a disturbance which prevents you from catching the rhythm of the music, or your mind and

> body might not be in step, or your partner might not harmonize with you. If in such cases you feel like venting your disappointment, but you do not, then you lose self-awareness, and become self-conscious.
>
> (1947/1969, p. 255)

Perls also provides this example:

> There is a story of a centipede who was asked which leg he moved first and how he managed to walk with all his legs at the same time. When he tried to do it deliberately he got so confused that he could not walk at all. Instead of merely becoming aware of his movements, he interfered with them.
>
> (1947/1969, p. 232)

Self-awareness consists of being fully present, in fluid and natural contact with oneself and the environment. Self-consciousness, on the other hand—which always involves retroflection, something unexpressed—consists of being focused on oneself rather than on the object of one's interest. It manifests as concern with one's image, insecurity, awkwardness, or embarrassment. According to Perls, self-awareness implies spontaneity, whereas self-consciousness, whose motor equivalent is clumsiness, represents its negation. Self-consciousness can be overcome by expressing what is inhibited and fully focusing on what arouses one's interest. Positive concentration, awareness, and spontaneity, therefore, are closely interconnected according to Perls.

3.2 The Spontaneous Self in *Gestalt Therapy*

The concept of spontaneity, according to Perls *et al.* (1994), has a specific meaning. It does not simply refer to the free expression of oneself. Spontaneity, the authors of *Gestalt Therapy* assert, is a "general quality of experience," understood in its fullness; it is an intrinsic quality of the integrated self.

As discussed in the previous chapter, in the optimal situation, according to Perls, Hefferline, and Goodman, the person is fully in contact with the environment, completely present in the here and now, and fully expresses their vital needs. In such conditions, the figure possesses specific qualities of clarity and brightness, while the background appears empty. In other words, the person is entirely absorbed by what sparks their interest, fully immersed in the experience they are living, as if, at that moment, nothing else existed for them.

For the authors of *Gestalt Therapy*, this optimal situation corresponds to the total functioning of the self, that is, to the spontaneous mode of experience, a middle ground between deliberateness (ego) and relaxation (id). In spontaneous experience, energy flows freely, enabling us to give our best:

> When one is in contact with the need and the circumstances, it is at once evident that reality is not something inflexible and unchangeable but is ready to be

> remade; and the more spontaneously one exercises every power of orientation and manipulation, without holding back, the more viable the remaking proves to be. Let anyone think of his own *best* strokes, in work or play, love or friendship, and see if this has not been the case.
>
> (Perls *et al.*, 1994, p. 23)

When we are fully focused on what we are doing, orientation (perceptual functions) and manipulation (motor functions) are therefore closely interconnected, forming together a unique and indivisible experience in its entirety. In such a state, we do not act because we feel something; rather, feeling and acting become one. The synaptic experience described by Erving and Miriam Polster is nothing more than the spontaneous experience in which orientation and manipulation unite. Polster and Polster write (1974, p. 215):

> One can sense this union if one becomes aware, for example, of his breathing while talking or of the flexibility of his body while moving or of his excitement while painting. At times of union between awareness and expression, profound feelings of presence and wholeness of personality, clarity of perception, and vibrancy of inner experience are common.

When orientation and manipulation form a unified experience, the resulting action is congruent, harmonious, and effective.

Clearly, spontaneous action is not always appropriate or effective; however, according to Perls *et al.* (1994), it enjoys certain privileged conditions. Being an expression of the organism's self-regulation, spontaneous action has the advantage of utilizing a large portion of the available energy and, therefore, appears "brighter, stronger, and shrewder" (p. 52). The authors write:

> Any other line of action that is presumed to be "better" must proceed with diminished power, less motivation, and more confused awareness; and must also involve devoting a certain amount of energy, and distracting a certain amount of attention, to keeping down the spontaneous self, which is seeking expression in self-regulation.
>
> (Perls *et al.*, 1994, p. 52)

Certainly, we cannot always be spontaneous; in some situations, inhibition is necessary. However, Perls, Hefferline, and Goodman caution: "Let us remember that to the extent to which we agree to situations in which self-regulation rarely operates, to that extent we must be content to live with diminished energy and brightness" (1994, p. 53).

Examples of spontaneous experiences frequently referenced by Perls, Hefferline, and Goodman include the artist's creative process and children's play. However, in their view, spontaneity is not the exclusive prerogative of artists or children: "Can the same middle of acceptance and growth operate in adult life in more 'serious' concerns? We believe so" (1994, p. 23). We can be spontaneous in all areas of our lives, regardless of the activity in which we are engaged.

In Gestalt therapy, the concept of spontaneity, which refers to the quality of action or expression, is closely connected to that of awareness, understood as the ability to be fully in contact with oneself and the environment. Spontaneity is an implicit aspect of awareness, a condition that integrates perception, movement, and feeling. The more aware we are, the better we can adapt creatively and spontaneously to what the environment presents to us.

Since, in optimal conditions, perceptual and motor functions form a functional unity, awareness and spontaneity are closely interrelated. Both terms describe the total and integrated functioning of the self, a mode of experience in which one is fully centered in the present moment, completely absorbed in what they are doing in the here and now.[2] However, they are not interchangeable: while awareness concerns "feeling" the present moment fully and represents the fundamental condition of experience, spontaneity manifests as the quality of action or expression that arises from it.

3.3 Therapist's Spontaneity in the Therapeutic Encounter

In Gestalt therapy, the therapeutic encounter constitutes a real situation in which the patient and therapist engage authentically in a delicate and complex interpersonal process that embodies the healing. Spagnuolo Lobb (2013, p. 37) writes:

> This implies that the Gestalt therapist immerses themselves fully in the relationship, that s/he uses their own self. The treatment is in fact based on two real people, who although they may also be revealed by means of techniques, stake themselves spontaneously, through their human limitations, in a relationship clearly defined by their complementary roles: one who gives the treatment and one who receives it.

In the encounter between patient and therapist, therefore, the therapist's ability to engage spontaneously, to "risk themselves" in the relationship (Perls *et al.*, 1994, p. 146), is crucial.

As previously discussed, spontaneity is linked to a state of full concentration and awareness. What enables the therapist to be spontaneous, to respond uniquely, personally, and sensitively, is being in deep contact with both the other and themselves. A significant example of the therapist's intense focus on the patient and the relationship is provided by Bianca Tarozzi (1994), who recounts the only therapy session she had with Isadore From:

> I went to From in 1978, on Susan Sontag's advice, because I was in New York and distressed as my sister was very ill. From then asked me to talk about my mother, and I said that I respected her because she was a woman who had

> suffered greatly: many of her close relatives had died under the bombings in Florence in September 1943. At this point, Isadore began to tremble very visibly. I pretended not to notice, and the session continued; I was leaving the next day [...]. In 1990, while translating one of his seminars in Venice, Isadore recounted that a patient had seen him tremble and, unlike me, had asked him why. Isadore had replied: "If the trembling bothers you, I can control it. But would you prefer that I focus on you or on my trembling?".
>
> (pp. 66–67)

The fundamental condition for the therapist's spontaneity essentially consists of being fully attuned to the patient, participating in their experience with no other goal in mind, and taking the risk of allowing the patient to perceive their emotional involvement. When the therapist is so focused on the patient's experience that it resonates deeply within them, in all their fibers, they spontaneously find, through self-regulation, the response capable of reaching the other. Their action then does not arise from cognitive elaboration or deliberate decision; rather, it is the immediate expression of their awareness. They do not act based on a preliminary assessment of the situation, nor with a predetermined final goal in mind. Totally absorbed in the situation, perceiving no separation between themselves and the other, unconcerned with doing the right thing, they are guided moment by moment by sensory perceptions, the flow of sensations, emotions, and intuitions co-created at the contact-boundary. They act immediately, guided by the flow of the present interaction. And their action is, for the most part, appropriate and effective. I believe that, understood in this way, spontaneity is the most important factor in therapeutic change.

The Polsters provide several examples of possible spontaneous actions by the therapist:

> He may hold his patient's hand while the patient is crying, refuse to answer questions that make him feel tricked, lend his patient money when he needs it, become sympathetically enraged when the patient has been wronged, tell a funny story when amused or tell the patient he or she is beautiful when the therapist sees it.
>
> (Polster & Polster, 1974, p. 19)

What unites the countless ways in which the therapist can express themselves personally and creatively is the quality of their presence. Only by being fully present with all their vitality at the contact-boundary can their action be truly spontaneous.

The right action at the right time can emerge only from the field, thanks to the therapist's awareness of what is happening at the contact-boundary moment by moment. Only if they are fully present can they grasp the intentionality of contact, which belongs not to the patient but to the co-created field in the present moment, and find the response that allows that intentionality to be realized. According to Spagnuolo Lobb (2013), supporting the intentionality that emerges from the field is not a technical intervention. Rather, it involves being in the co-created situation consciously and spontaneously, providing the patient with the specific relational confirmation they need in the here and now. The aim of therapy is the spontaneity of the encounter, in which the shared intentionality in the current situation is realized. A full and spontaneous encounter thus becomes a moment of transformation.

By engaging in the relationship "man to man," as the authors of *Gestalt Therapy* state (Perls *et al.*, 1994, p. 25), the therapist not only facilitates the other's change but also grants themselves the opportunity to change and grow, experiencing the richness and vitality of the encounter.

3.4 Spontaneity, Competence, and Responsibility

How does one learn to engage in relationships spontaneously? This question is challenging to answer. Certainly, a therapist must possess inherent qualities. Only with this foundation can they develop the ability to be spontaneous, primarily through training, experience, and supervision.

Spontaneity, as understood in Gestalt therapy, requires adequate awareness and mature therapeutic competence. Spagnuolo Lobb (2003, p. 37) writes:

> Improvisational co-creation demands that the partners are present and alive at the contact boundary: it is similar to the sophisticated ability of the jazz player who has all the musical knowledge in her blood and is able to be fresh, strong, contactful, and unique in her playing.

Only when the therapist embodies the necessary competence—gained through professional training and clinical experience—can they possess the attention, sensitivity, and intuition to perceive what occurs at the contact-boundary and take the appropriate action at the right moment.

Meditation can also serve as a valuable tool for therapists to cultivate their ability to be fully present in relationships. The concentration experiments suggested by Perls *et al.* (1994) to enhance awareness are quite similar to forms of meditation. In my opinion, we should encourage our students to practice regular meditation to develop their capacity to engage at the contact-boundary sensitively and spontaneously.

When a therapist can be fully present in the here and now and possesses the necessary competence, they can derive valuable guidance from the sensations and emotions that emerge in their awareness moment by moment during interactions with others. Their immediate experience can thus become the most important therapeutic tool at their disposal. The therapist may choose to verbalize how the patient's expressions resonate within them or may express their emotional involvement directly and spontaneously through non-verbal means. The immediate and direct expression of the therapist's feelings through non-verbal and implicit channels can have a more profound impact on the patient than verbalizing their feelings, especially if the latter results from an intellectually mediated choice rather than genuine spontaneity. However, if the therapist is truly present at the contact-boundary, perceiving what emerges from the field and communicating it to the patient—though a technical intervention—can also be highly effective. The Polsters provide the following example of a therapist verbalizing their immediate experience: "Using his own reactivity, when the patient's voice grates harshly, he may say, 'You make me feel like a naughty child'" (Polster & Polster, 1974, p. 18).

At times, however, the therapist may refrain from expressing their feelings, sensing that the patient may not be able to handle it. But, as the Polsters caution, retroflection should not become a habitual mode for the therapist, who

> can only afford a limited amount of such tithes and should offer them sparingly. The taxes become too high, though, when he risks losing the effervescence which he senses when he is functioning best. Like a cat preening himself or a safe-cracker who sandpapers his fingertips, the therapist has to keep himself honed.
>
> (1974, p. 22)

The therapist's immediate experience is their most fundamental tool, and they must always consider both the other person's feelings and their own.

The Polsters also warn of the risks associated with misunderstanding spontaneity. Spontaneity, merely as the free expression of the therapist's feelings, does not guarantee therapeutic effectiveness. Spontaneity must always be accompanied by responsibility. The therapist's free expression would be simply childish if not coupled with the assumption of responsibility for its consequences. Polster and Polster (1974, p. 21) write:

> Whatever we do, there is always a next moment. Evading responsibility in the next moment is a way of depersonalizing. Although it allows a surface freedom, it also puts up a wall through lack of genuine concern between any two people and certainly between patient and therapist.

The responsibility inherent in the therapist's caregiving role is an intrinsic aspect of the therapeutic situation, even when they engage spontaneously. Without responsibility and the ethical commitment that the therapeutic relationship entails, the therapist's free expression becomes impulsive, reckless, and potentially harmful.[3]

3.5 The Main Modes of the Self in the Therapeutic Situation

The therapist, of course, cannot operate exclusively in a spontaneous manner, relying solely on their own sensations, intuitions, and creative improvisation. In the therapeutic situation, the four main modes of the self—spontaneity, deliberateness, relaxation, and autonomy—alternately and continuously integrate in response to the needs of the moment. The shift from one to another can happen involuntarily and spontaneously or through a deliberate and conscious choice. For much of the session, the therapist might let their attention wander freely, adopting an attitude of maximum openness and receptivity to everything they perceive and experience. In this state, they operate in the id mode of the self, characterized by relaxation and unfocused attention. Later, they may transition to a different mode of the self, if the situation demands it.

For example, a patient with borderline personality disorder says: "I feel like a hollow trunk!" This expression deeply affects the therapist, causing a sensation of tightness in their stomach, blocking their breath. They feel intense tension in their body, tighten their lips, and utter a sound: "Mhmm." They think: "Wow! Is this how it feels?" After a brief pause, during which the patient and the therapist exchange a silent gaze, the patient resumes describing their feelings of intense anguish. In this case, the therapist reacts immediately and authentically to the patient's words, letting their sensations and emotions emerge without filtering or excessively analyzing the situation. Their spontaneous reaction, expressed through a guttural sound and intense eye contact, creates a moment of genuine, profound connection with the patient. This type of response exemplifies the spontaneous mode of the self, in which the therapist, fully present in the here and now and reacting authentically, fosters a moment of intimate connection with the patient, allowing the therapeutic process to develop.

The following example illustrates a mode of deliberate response from the therapist. A patient says, "I wonder how it will be when the time comes to end the therapy." The therapist reflects on the meaning of this statement, which brings up the theme of separation at a critical stage in the process. They wonder whether the patient is still dependent and fears an early end to therapy, or if, feeling stronger and more autonomous, they are beginning to explore their relationship with the idea of closure. The therapist then decides to propose an experiment: "How do you imagine the last session? Try to fantasize about how it will unfold." In this case, they consider various possible interpretations—such as the patient's dependence or a growing sense of autonomy—and, based on this assessment, they choose the most appropriate intervention. This process of reflection, evaluation, and conscious decision-making is characteristic of the deliberate mode of the self, which guides the therapist in the targeted use of their skills.

In the following example, the therapist's intervention is based on the autonomous mode of the self. A patient recounts a dream they had after the last session: "I dreamed of being in a precarious elevator. While the elevator ascended, I feared falling at any moment."

For a therapist who habitually adopts Isadore From's approach, interpreting dreams as forms of retroflection related to the therapeutic relationship, an intervention like: "How did I make you feel in danger during the last session?" feels almost natural. This intervention represents an application of the autonomous mode of the self, in which the therapist confidently uses acquired skills that are an integral part of their therapeutic style and identity.

All modes of the self are necessary, both in psychotherapy and in daily life. Psychological health implies the ability to fluidly transition between them based on the demands of the situation, finding a harmonious balance among them.

Spontaneity, in particular, plays a crucial role in the therapeutic process. Asking to what extent the therapist can express themselves spontaneously in the encounter with the patient is not much different, at least in some respects, from asking to what extent spontaneity is possible and practicable in life. To this latter question, Perls *et al.* (1994, p. 53) respond: "We believe immensely more than we deliberately allow in the now; people can be much brighter and more energetic than they are, and then they would also be shrewder."

Notes

1 Already published in *Quaderni di Gestalt*, 2015, XXVIII, 2: 79–93. https://doi.org/10.3280/GEST2015-002004.

2 It is interesting to note that the concept of *flow*, proposed by Mihaly Csikszentmihalyi (1975), shows notable similarities to the concept of the spontaneous self described by Perls, Hefferline, and Goodman. Csikszentmihalyi defines *flow* as an experiential state in which a person becomes so deeply focused on the activity they are performing that they lose their sense of time, self, and the surrounding reality, describing this experience as a current of water that carries them along. Perls *et al.* (1994), however, describe the spontaneous experience not only as a feeling of being "carried along," but also as being "engaged" in it (pp. 154, 161). This highlights an additional dimension of active and conscious participation, enriching the comparison between the two concepts.

3 On the topic of ethics in Gestalt therapy, Dan Bloom (2013) introduces the concept of *situated ethics*. Drawing from European phenomenology and existentialism, Bloom views situated ethics as a fundamental disposition toward others, serving as the foundation for any determination of right and wrong. This situated ethics is an integral part of the situational structure, inherent in the human condition of *being with others*.

References

Bloom, D. (2013). Situated ethics and the ethical world of Gestalt therapy. In G. Francesetti, M. Gecele, & J. Roubal (Eds.), *Gestalt therapy in clinical practice: From psychopathology to the aesthetics of contact* (pp. 131–146). Milano: FrancoAngeli.

Csikszentmihalyi, M. (1975). *Beyond boredom and anxiety: Experiencing flow in work and play*. San Francisco, CA: Jossey-Bass.

Macaluso, M. A. (2015). La spontaneità dell'incontro terapeutico come fattore chiave di cambiamento. *Quaderni di Gestalt*, 28(2), 79–93. https://doi.org/10.3280/GEST2015-002005

Perls, F. (1969). *Ego, hunger and aggression: The beginning of Gestalt therapy*. New York: Vintage Books (Random House).(Original work published 1947).

Perls, F., Hefferline, R., & Goodman, P. (1951/1994). *Gestalt therapy: Excitement and growth in the human personality*. Highland, NY: The Gestalt Journal Press.

Polster, E., & Polster, M. (1974). *Gestalt therapy integrated: Contours of theory and practice*. New York, NY: Vintage Books.

Spagnuolo Lobb, M. (2003). Therapeutic meeting as improvisational co-creation. In M. Spagnuolo Lobb & N. Amendt-Lyon (Eds.), *Creative license: The art of Gestalt therapy* (pp. 37–49). Wien/New York, NY: Springer.

Spagnuolo Lobb, M. (2013). *The now-for-next in psychotherapy: Gestalt therapy recounted in post-modern society*. Milano: FrancoAngeli. (Original work published 2011 as *Il now-for-next in psicoterapia*, Milano: FrancoAngeli).

Tarozzi B. (1994). Diario di una traduttrice. *Quaderni di Gestalt*, 18/19: 65–67.

Chapter 4

Deliberateness and Spontaneity in Gestalt Therapeutic Action[1]

4.1 Introduction

In recent decades, the focus of Gestalt therapy has shifted from the individual-centered model to the relational model. This theoretical shift has led to an evolution in Gestalt clinical practice, which today emphasizes the healing power of the therapeutic relationship rather than the exploration of the patient's experience. The growing interest in the relational perspective has led to the replacement of traditional therapeutic action, aimed at developing awareness through the use of techniques and experiments, with dialogue and the spontaneous encounter between patient and therapist.

The question that guides this work, which describes some modes of Gestalt therapeutic action, is the following: in contemporary relational Gestalt therapy, is there still room for the classical theoretical and clinical framework, centered on the individual and the use of techniques? To try to answer this question, which involves multiple aspects, I will first refer to the conception of subjectivity in Gestalt therapy, which I have already discussed in the first chapter of this book. From this conception, in fact, derives the choice of its object of study: the individual and/or the relationship. Next, I will distinguish between two aspects of Gestalt therapeutic action, one deliberate and the other spontaneous. Deliberate therapeutic action includes both work on the patient's individual experience and work on the therapeutic relationship. Spontaneous therapeutic action, on the other hand, refers to the co-created therapeutic encounter.

In deliberate work on the relationship, the exploration of what happens between the patient and therapist on a predominantly verbal and explicit level constitutes the fundamental tool for change. The very idea of "work" implies a deliberate action, in which the therapist refers to a methodology. In spontaneous therapeutic activity, which primarily concerns the implicit level of the relationship, change, however, comes from the experience of the encounter between patient and therapist. In this case, the focus is on the co-created relationship through moments of mutual recognition and intimate contact, in which the therapist engages in a personal and authentic way.

The use of the term "relationship" within the Gestalt discourse requires clarification, as it is often conflated with the concept of "contact." Perls *et al.* (1994)

DOI: 10.4324/9781003726753-5

focus on contact—defined as the interaction that occurs in the present moment—rather than on the broader concept of 'relationship' as it develops over time. The model of Perls, Hefferline, and Goodman is centered on the here and now and does not specifically address what evolves between two people through their successive encounters. If we consider the interpersonal situation from a temporal perspective, we can distinguish between contact, which is the immediate interaction between two people, and the relationship, which is the complex of contacts that have occurred between them over time, shaping their ongoing connection.

4.2 Subjective Experience According to the Perls, Hefferline, and Goodman Model

Gestalt therapy, as affirmed by Perls *et al.* (1994), focuses on the phenomenology of awareness. Its object of study is the subjective experience of the present moment (or the self), conceived not as an internal process of the psyche but as a function of the organism/environment field.

Perls, Hefferline, and Goodman use the concept of the field to emphasize that the individual and the environment form an inseparable unity. The primary reality is not composed of two separate entities but of a single indivisible totality: the field, which includes both. Subjective experience is therefore a function of this field. In the therapeutic context, patient and therapist co-create the present situation: neither can be considered in isolation, as both constitute a unified whole within the field to which they belong. The object of study in Gestalt therapy is, therefore, the individual–environment unit.

Although the model of Perls, Hefferline, and Goodman is centered on the individual, it stands as an alternative to the intrapsychic perspective, which views the mind as an isolated entity. Gestalt therapy studies the individual not for themselves, but as closely and indissolubly connected to their environment. Experience is a relational and interactive process, not merely an internal construction. The relationship between the individual and the environment exists even before personal experience and contributes to shaping it. Individual subjectivity exists only within the process of contact, which constitutes it in the here and now, in a continuous becoming, moment by moment. Outside of the relational process that allows it to express and actualize itself in the here and now, subjective experience—the internal world—is nothing but an abstraction, something that lacks reality.

Affirming the inherently relational nature of experience does not imply, of course, that the object of study in Gestalt therapy must be exclusively the interaction between patient and therapist. The subjective individual experience of the patient is also a focus of study, but as a function of the field, that is, always keeping in mind that it takes shape and acquires meaning within the experience of contact with the other, in a co-created field. While exploring the subjective experience of the patient, the therapist maintains a global vision of the field, also considering their own role and influence on the patient's experience and on the therapeutic relationship.

4.3 Deliberateness and Spontaneity in Therapeutic Action

Referring to Perls *et al.* (1994), who identify deliberateness and spontaneity as two fundamental modalities of self-functioning, unduly separated by our neurotic culture, I distinguish two forms of Gestalt therapeutic activity: one deliberate and the other spontaneous. These two modalities should not be considered as separate dimensions of the clinical situation but rather as integrated aspects of therapeutic action.[2]

According to Perls, Hefferline, and Goodman, deliberateness represents the active and voluntary modality characteristic of the ego, the partial functioning of the self dedicated to identification. Spontaneity, on the other hand, is the integrated and total functioning of the self, reflecting a condition of experiential fullness. In the deliberate modality, experience is differentiated into objects, which are known through abstract rationality; in the spontaneous modality, organism and environment are in confluence (from the Latin "confluere", meaning "to flow together"), and reality is grasped in its immediacy.

When the therapist acts deliberately, the other becomes an object of observation and study. Perls *et al.* (1994, p. 91) write: "When things and other persons have once become outlined and abstracted objects, they can enter into useful deliberate fixed and habitual relations with the self." In this case, the therapist draws on their theoretical and methodological knowledge: they evaluate the situation according to a reference model, identify a goal, develop a plan to achieve it, and act accordingly. As Perls, Hefferline, and Goodman suggest, orientation (diagnostic evaluation) and manipulation (therapeutic intervention) constitute distinct moments of the process. Furthermore, the therapist is self-aware, observing and evaluating themselves.

When acting spontaneously, however, the therapist experiences a sense of engagement and full attunement with the other. They evaluate the situation as it unfolds and respond immediately, unmediated by their theoretical or technical knowledge. In this case, the therapist does not have a clear goal or endpoint but intuitively directs their actions in accordance with what emerges moment by moment at the contact-boundary. When therapeutic action is spontaneous, it is not "something one knows beforehand, but something one does and then knows and can talk about" (Perls *et al.*, 1994, p. 175). Orientation and manipulation are integrated, and perception and action merge into a unified whole. Fully immersed in the experience, "engaged in the situation" to the point of losing a sense of self, the therapist feels that their action does not stem from conscious effort but unfolds naturally, almost as if developing on its own. Such an action is likely to be effective because it represents "a spontaneous response to an actuality" (Perls *et al.*, 1994, p. 224).

Deliberate therapeutic activity includes everything the therapist does intentionally to help the patient achieve a new creative adjustment. In contrast, spontaneous activity manifests in the personal, unpremeditated actions of the therapist or the patient, leading both to moments of mutual recognition and intimate contact that transform their relationship.

When acting deliberately, the therapist observes the process from an external perspective and employs techniques. By "technique," I mean any intervention or action the therapist performs deliberately, based on a theoretical and methodological model, with the goal of producing therapeutic effects.[3]

When acting spontaneously, however, the therapist is fully engaged in the process, responding immediately and unpremeditatedly to what emerges in the present moment. Fully in contact with the situation, they trust the spontaneous self-regulation of the field and express themselves in a personal and creative way. In this case, the focus of change is no longer the therapist's deliberate action but the spontaneous encounter with the patient.

By acting intentionally, the therapist directs the therapeutic process to some extent and feels secure, relying on their theoretical and clinical knowledge. This enables them to know what to do, when to do it, and why. Acting spontaneously, on the other hand, the therapist accepts the risk of "deconstructing" themselves by engaging in an intimate interpersonal process in which their acquired knowledge takes a back seat, and they can only orient themselves through their ability to live fully in the present moment and perceive what is happening at the contact-boundary, moment by moment.

Only deliberate therapeutic action can be taught and learned, as it is based on theoretical and methodological models. The ability of the therapist to act spontaneously, however, is the result of a combination of factors: their personal qualities, their own psychotherapy journey, the clinical experience gained over time, their existential path, and, in some cases, the practice of meditation.

According to Perls *et al.* (1994), deliberateness and spontaneity are not in opposition but rather represent two complementary and integrated dimensions of self-functioning. The dichotomy between these two modalities is, in fact, the result of a neurotic split. We can therefore consider deliberate and spontaneous therapeutic action as opposite poles of a continuum, along which all possible gradations and combinations of both aspects are positioned. In every intervention or therapist response, there are varying degrees of both deliberateness and spontaneity. The therapeutic relationship, like any flexible and healthy relationship, requires the ability to move along the intentionality/spontaneity spectrum according to the needs of the moment.

4.4 Deliberate Therapeutic Activity

In the context of deliberate therapeutic activity, we can distinguish between work focused on the individual, centered on the patient's subjective experience, and relational work, which concerns the exchange that occurs between the patient and the therapist in the here and now.

This distinction between individual work and relational work represents a methodological choice and does not undermine the unified perspective of Gestalt therapy. In the Gestalt view, individual and relational aspects are not opposing concepts but two facets of the same reality: the present situation. We can choose to analyze this reality from either perspective, as both ultimately lead to equivalent outcomes. Individual work on awareness enhances the patient's relational competence, while relational work fosters their awareness.

Both individual-focused work and work oriented toward the therapeutic relationship always rely on a specific methodology and simultaneously require constant attention to the field. In the following paragraphs, I will examine the essential aspects of Gestalt methodology and briefly outline the different modalities of individual and relational therapeutic work.

4.4.1 The Gestalt Methodology

The fundamental method of classical Gestalt therapy is the phenomenological exploration of present-moment experience. This exploration can take place through the therapist's questions, the patient's concentration, or experimentation.

Perls *et al.* (1994, p. 312) state that "the actual situation is organized in a way that is detailed, structured, vivid, concernful." They define therapy as "analyzing the internal structure of the actual experience" (1994, p. 8). This analysis involves systematically focusing on the *how* of experience, its various aspects, details, and implications. It entails breaking the experience into parts (de-structuring) and subsequently reuniting them creatively (re-structuring). This process allows one "to change the conditions and provide other grounds of experience, till the self discovers-and-invents the figure" (1994, p. 213). Experience changes when its conditions change, that is, when the background from which it emerges shifts. Phenomenological exploration modifies the background, enabling a new figure to emerge.

According to Perls, Hefferline, and Goodman, attempting to directly modify a patient's dysfunctional belief would mean going against their subjective reality and way of seeing things, generating resistance. To change such a belief, it is necessary instead to explore in detail, through a series of targeted questions, the many aspects that constitute their background, i.e., the overall context. Attention is therefore directed not to the figure but to the elements of its background. This approach, referred to by the authors of *Gestalt Therapy* as the *contextual method*, is based on the continuous and thorough analysis of the many dimensions of the background of current experience. Such focus leads to a new organization of experience, a different awareness that translates into a new perspective and different behaviors.[4]

The exploration of experience can be carried out not only by the therapist through targeted questions but also by the patient themselves, by concentration on some aspect of their current experience. Perls (1947/1969) conceived of concentration as a state akin to meditation and regarded it as a highly effective technique capable of fostering the evolution and transformation of experience. In *Gestalt Therapy*, concentration is described as the foundational technique of Gestalt therapy. The second volume of the foundational text is devoted to a series of concentration techniques and exercises aimed at developing awareness. A particularly significant application of concentration is the continuum of awareness, which consists of noticing and verbalizing what emerges to awareness moment by moment.

After the initial phase of establishing Gestalt therapy, concentration exercises were gradually replaced by Gestalt experiments, which contributed to the global recognition of Gestalt therapy, albeit sometimes in a partial or stereotyped manner. The Gestalt experiment involves inviting the patient to try something that represents a new experience for them, developed collaboratively with the therapist through dialogue. Rather than aiming for immediate change, the experiment serves as an essential tool for exploring the patient's experience, allowing for a deeper understanding of their difficulties. In this regard, Perls *et al.* (1994, Introduction, p. xxx) write: "With this method we bring to the surface the difficulties of the patient. Not the task, but what interferes with the successful completion of the task becomes the center of our work."

According to Wheeler (1991), we primarily owe the Gestalt conception of change as the reorganization of experience to Goodman's contribution. Perls, on the other hand, always considered the expression of repressed emotions, which allows for the release of energy and the reintegration of dissociated parts, as a fundamental factor in change. In this regard, Perls (1947/1969, p. 235) writes: "Every picture admitted, every tear shed, puts a bit of energy at the disposal of your conscious personality." From Perls's perspective, all work on developing awareness through phenomenological exploration and experiments aims at authentic self-expression and the integration of fragmented parts of the personality. This perspective, complementary to Goodman's, emphasizes the importance of emotional integration as a prerequisite for change and for the creative reorganization of experience.

A fundamental aspect of Gestalt methodology is the work on body awareness, considered the primary foundation of human experience. In this context, Kepner (1993) and Frank (2001) have explored the role of the body in Gestalt therapy in complementary ways. Kepner examines bodily processes as tools for developing awareness, while Frank, drawing on the teachings of Laura Perls, analyzes the evolution of body language from a relational perspective.

Kepner (1993) proposes a model of bodywork based on the contact cycle developed by the Cleveland Gestalt Institute. This approach focuses on fostering awareness, promoting the experience of the body as an essential and integrated component of the self.

Frank (2001), building on Laura Perls' clinical approach, adopts an evolutionary and relational perspective to explore bodily experience. She examines infant movement patterns, highlighting their crucial role in the psychological development of the child. These patterns, which remain an integral part of the contact process in adulthood, become interpretative tools for understanding phenomena that emerge in the therapeutic relationship, providing valuable insights for both diagnosis and therapeutic intervention.

Together, the contributions of Kepner and Frank underscore the central role of the body in Gestalt therapy, both as a gateway to individual experience and as a means to facilitate more authentic and spontaneous contact modalities.

4.4.2 Working on the Individual

The work focused on the individual is the phenomenological exploration of the patient's subjective experience. It may involve working on an aspect of the experience that openly emerges in the here and now, such as a clenched jaw, a slight change in voice, a particular mode of contact, or any other element that catches the therapist's attention.

For Gestalt therapy, the current situation—what happens in the here and now of the session—represents the privileged context for clinical work. This means that the phenomenological exploration of the patient's experience primarily concerns "his attitude towards himself and towards the therapist" in the present moment. However, this does not exclude the possibility of including "his ordinary behavior in family, sex, job" (Perls *et al.*, 1994, p. 64). Material from the patient's daily life and the problems it presents may also be an integral part of the therapeutic work, provided it serves to achieve a new creative adjustment in the here and now.

According to Perls *et al.* (1994), therapy is not about recovering something from the past or predicting what lies ahead in the future but about completing the Gestalt in the current situation. Gestalt therapy shifts the focus from the past to the present—not to ignore past wounds but to work through them via the present moment, the only space where real change and healing can occur. The emphasis on the here and now does not, however, exclude the past and future from therapeutic work, as both contribute to shaping the current organization of experience. To the extent that they manifest in the present and influence the current reality, the past and future become relevant: "Memory and anticipation are acts in the present, and it is important for us to analyze their place in the structure of the actuality" (1994, p. 67).

Attention to the patient's history, and even work on the past, does not conflict with the theoretical foundations of Gestalt therapy but rather with a certain stereotyped image of it. The authors of *Gestalt Therapy* recommend a flexible and non-rigid application of its principles, emphasizing that, depending on the situation, even tools like interpretation and work on the past can be useful if they lead to a new creative adjustment in the here and now. As Perls *et al.* write:

> It is absurd to think even for a moment of not combating the resistances, of not rousing anxiety, of not showing that a neurotic response does not work, of not reviving the past, of withholding all interpretation and discarding one's science. [...] The problem then comes down to the detailed one of what is the structure of the interview: how to employ and deploy the conflict, the anxiety, the past, the conception and the interpretation, in order to reach the climax of creative adjustment?
>
> (Perls *et al.*, 1994, p. 63)

In conclusion, any method can be useful, provided it enables the patient to achieve awareness and integration that allow them to live fully in the present.

4.4.3 *Working on the Relationship*

What happens in the here and now of the therapeutic relationship is interpreted by Perls, Hefferline, and Goodman not as a mere repetition of past relational patterns but as "a real social situation." Contrasting the Gestalt method with the psychoanalytic one, the authors state: "The transference (emotional relation to the analyst) is construed as the reliving of the childhood events, when the simple facts of the current situation are sufficient to account for whatever happens, without reference to the past at all" (Perls *et al.*, 1994, pp. 465–466). Working on the relationship involves analyzing the structure of the dialogue in the here and now, focusing on the experiences, both of the patient and the therapist, that emerge in their current interaction. The exploration of what occurs between the patient and the therapist constitutes the technical aspect of relationship work. This aspect does not exclude the therapist's personal involvement. On the contrary, the therapist pays attention to what the patient experiences in the here and now of the relationship while simultaneously engaging and presenting themselves in a personal and authentic way. Both the patient and the therapist are involved in a dialogue where they contribute their different experiences and their individual ways of being in the relationship, striving to create shared meanings and a common representation of "reality." This dialogical exchange becomes the fundamental tool for understanding and modifying how the patient organizes their subjective experience and their encounter with others. The confrontation between the subjective experiences of the patient and the therapist triggers transformative processes not only in the patient but also in the therapist.

A method frequently used in Gestalt therapy is one developed by Isadore From, which consists of bringing what the patient expresses back to the here and now of the therapeutic relationship. This method is embodied in the question the therapist asks the patient: "How do I contribute to your experience in the here and now?" For instance, if the patient reports feeling anxious, the therapist might ask, "How do I contribute to your anxiety?" From this perspective, even when the patient talks about a dream, a film, or an event that happened the day before (or even a month earlier), they do so because that content carries a message about the here and now of their relationship with the therapist. The therapist's focus is not on the content itself but on the interpersonal contact occurring in the present moment through the communication of that content. The theoretical premise of this technique is that what the patient expresses is not merely an expression of their inner world but also a reflection of the relational field.

This technique is commonly considered a way of working on the relationship. However, it does not necessarily always involve this. The therapist might connect the patient's experience to the here and now of their relationship, inviting the patient to interact directly with them, but without personally engaging in exploring the current situation. In this case, the therapeutic work does not focus on the relationship but rather on the patient's subjective experience, mediated through the relationship. Here is an example:

Patient (P): "I often find that, when I'm with others, I don't feel completely at ease."

Therapist (T): "And with me, in what way do you not feel completely at ease?"

P: "With you? I don't know... Maybe because I see you as an authoritative person, superior to me, and that makes me feel a bit intimidated."

T: "If you didn't feel so intimidated by me, what would you want to do or say?"

P: "I don't know..."

T "Take a moment to think about it."

P: "Well, I think I'd ask you some questions... I'd like to know more about you, your life..."

T: "Do you want to try asking me something you're curious about?"

P: "Umm... Are you married? Do you have children?"

T: "How do you feel asking me these things?"

In this case, the therapist uses the present relationship to explore some of the patient's habitual contact patterns and support them in addressing what holds them back, but without personally engaging in the exchange. The therapeutic action focuses solely on the patient's individual experience. Only when the therapist questions themselves, exploring how they contribute to creating the current situation, does the intervention become relational work. In the brief exchange that follows, the therapist adopts a relational work approach:

P: "I don't feel your interest in me."

T: "What gave you the impression that I'm not interested in you?"

P: "I can't say exactly, but I have this feeling."

T: "I wonder: is it that you don't perceive my interest in you, or is it that I'm not expressing it enough?"

Not everything a patient brings to a session directly concerns the patient–therapist relationship or can be related to it, even if it takes shape within that context. In some situations, it may be more useful to consider the experience as belonging to the patient rather than linking it to the current relationship. For example, a patient might tell the therapist about the embarrassment she felt when her father showed her ambiguous attention. In this case, the patient's primary need could be to express her pain and anger within the safe environment of the therapeutic relationship. The therapist might then choose to simply listen attentively and empathetically, facilitating the expression of her intense emotions.

On the other hand, if the therapist perceives a certain discomfort in the relational field, he might decide to shift the focus to the present interaction, asking: "What is it about me that makes you feel embarrassed?" In this case, the patient's predominant need—her intentionality of contact—could be to test the therapist's reliability, to ensure that his interest is genuine and not ambiguous, thereby feeling secure enough to reveal her more vulnerable parts.

4.4.4 The Dialogical Attitude

Since the late 1980s, a specifically relational orientation has developed within Gestalt therapy, emphasizing dialogue as a fundamental tool for fostering awareness. As Yontef (2002) highlights, this approach is grounded in the principles of dialogue, which are rooted in Martin Buber's (1958) philosophy. These principles can be summarized in three key elements: *inclusion*, *presence*, and *dialogical availability*.

The concept of *inclusion*, which is closely related to empathy, refers to the ability to enter another person's world and understand their experience without losing contact with one's own perspective. It is not a unilateral process but a reciprocal dynamic in which we welcome the other into ourselves while allowing ourselves to be welcomed by them. This exchange enables the patient to feel understood and to receive profound validation of their uniqueness and value.

Presence is the capacity to be fully available and authentic in an encounter, actively participating and allowing oneself to be deeply involved without reservation. It involves complete immersion in the relationship in the present moment, a mutual exchange in which both parties perceive and reveal themselves in their authenticity.

Dialogical availability—though not a term directly used by Buber—refers to the therapist's ability to remain open and receptive to what emerges in the dialogue. This attitude requires a willingness to set aside prejudices, rigid patterns, and personal intentions, trusting the spontaneity of the relational process. The therapist does not impose direction but remains ready to enter the patient's world, respecting their pace and lived experience.

In Gestalt therapy, phenomenologically oriented toward relationship and dialogue, the therapist is committed to deeply understanding the patient's subjective experience, creating a safe and authentic space where the patient can feel accepted. The therapist engages in a reciprocal exchange characterized by openness, transparency, and respect, avoiding any position of superiority.

The therapist does not pursue predetermined objectives or attempt to directly alter the patient's experience. Instead, they embrace what emerges at the contact-boundary, respecting the patient's process and acknowledging their own limitations. Additionally, they demonstrate genuine willingness to correct themselves and learn through dialogue.

Here is a brief example.

P: "I felt hostility in what you said."

T: "Perhaps what I said came across as rejection or aggression. I can understand how it might have seemed aggressive to you. It's possible you picked up on a part of my experience of which I wasn't aware. What I am aware of, however, is that my intention was to show you a different perspective."

Later, the therapist might add: "You're helping me clarify what happened. I didn't realize that my way of being might have made you feel rejected."

When we talk about the principles of dialogue, we refer not to a methodology but to a fundamental attitude—a way of being that can give rise to both technical interventions and spontaneous responses. One example of applying these principles is *self-disclosure*, the deliberate choice of the therapist to share their subjective experience with the patient. This represents a technical application of the principle of *presence*.

On the other hand, the therapist's immediate expression of involvement, arising from their awareness of the field and leading to a moment of mutual recognition, constitutes a spontaneous response. Such a response is not planned but emerges naturally from the interaction in the here and now.

4.4.5 Integrating Classical Techniques into the Relational Perspective

The Gestalt therapist has access to a wide range of techniques and intervention methods, enabling effective work on both individual experience and relational dynamics. A significant example is represented by the different approaches to dreamwork, which the therapist can choose based on the situation at hand and their therapeutic style. For instance, they might decide to focus on the relationship, following Isadore From's approach, which viewed dreams as attempts to resolve disruptions in the contact-boundary between patient and therapist. Alternatively, the therapist might opt for Fritz Perls' method, interpreting dreams as projections of alienated parts of the self, thereby working on the patient's individual experience. Another option is to work on dreams through *concentration*, a technique used by Perls and his wife, Laura, in the groups they led in New York during the early years of Gestalt therapy. This approach will be explored in Chapter 6.

These different ways of working with dreams show how classical Gestalt techniques can be used for different purposes. This raises a central question: to what extent can these techniques be integrated into the current relational perspective? According to Yontef, the use of classical Gestalt techniques, focused on the individual, can be compatible with the current relational Gestalt orientation, provided the therapist adopts an authentically dialogical attitude. Conversely, these techniques are inconsistent with the relational approach of contemporary Gestalt therapy when used to pursue predetermined goals or to directly induce change in the patient, rather than fostering a therapeutic process based on open exploration and the spontaneous development of experience in the here and now. On this matter, Yontef (2002) writes:

> Insight into cognition, body process, interruptions to awareness and contact can go hand-in-hand with inclusion and phenomenological focusing – or can be a form of behavior modification, that is the therapist being a change agent trying to cure the patient. I do not consider the latter good Gestalt therapy or consistent with basic Gestalt therapy principles.
>
> (pp. 25–26)

At times, Yontef observes, there still persists, albeit subtly and implicitly, an attitude in Gestalt practice aimed at frustrating what may be interpreted as dependency needs or attempts at manipulation by the patient. This attitude, typical of the therapeutic style of Gestalt therapy in the 1960s, often evokes feelings of humiliation and shame in the patient, clearly contradicting the fundamental principles of the relational and dialogical approach of contemporary Gestalt therapy.

In my view, the new relational perspective can integrate the traditional individual-centered perspective, enriching our theoretical and clinical framework. Classical techniques are not eliminated by the relational approach but are instead contextualized and placed within a broader framework. The therapist must evaluate the situation at hand and decide whether to focus on what is happening in the therapeutic relationship or on the patient's individual experience.

However, attention to the field must always remain a priority. Even when exploring the patient's subjective experience, the Gestalt therapist stays attuned to the relational context from which it emerges. As Yontef aptly warns (2002, p. 23): "Every intervention, every moment of therapy, is not only a technical event but also a moment of interpersonal contact." Ultimately, every therapeutic intervention must be understood in the light of field dynamics, recognizing that technique alone is never sufficient—interpersonal contact is what determines its effectiveness.

4.5 Spontaneous Therapeutic Activity

Spontaneous therapeutic activity is the process of co-creating the therapeutic relationship, which develops through moments of mutual recognition and sharing. The therapist contributes to this process through their way of being, through the ability to engage authentically and personally in the situation.

In spontaneous therapeutic activity, change does not arise from exploring what happens within the relationship but from the direct and lived experience of the present encounter. In this case, therapeutic action coincides with the very experience of the encounter between patient and therapist.

4.5.1 Differences Between Deliberate Relational Activity and Spontaneous Relational Activity

Deliberate work on the relationship involves, as we have seen, the exploration of what happens at the contact-boundary between two interacting individuals, who remain distinct. Although this dialogue may also involve implicit and nonverbal aspects, relational work primarily focuses on explicit, conscious, and verbal communication.[5]

Spontaneous activity, on the other hand, occurs primarily at an implicit level and involves those particular moments of full contact and mutual attunement, where, even if only for an instant, the distinction between "I" and "You" seems to soften, creating a sense of profound connection. When working on the relationship, the therapist aims for a shared verbal understanding of who is doing what to whom. Acting spontaneously, however, the therapist engages with the patient in the unfolding experience, fully immersing in the shared moment. In such cases, there is no need for explicit reflection on what happened at the contact-boundary afterward.

Here's an example: a patient feels irritated because she perceives that the therapist does not fully grasp the intensity of her suffering and tends to downplay her distress. The therapist asks her how she felt unseen in her pain and works with her to understand how both contributed to this dynamic. Through this exploration, they realize that the therapist was misled by the patient's strengths and resources, while the patient had not fully expressed her pain and anguish. This is an example of deliberate work on the relationship.

In contrast, the following is an example of spontaneous therapeutic activity: the patient expresses anger toward the therapist. The therapist, believing the anger to be justified, apologizes. Alternatively, the therapist, feeling their own anger appropriate to the situation, expresses it in turn. In both cases, the therapist's immediate, personal, and spontaneous response—an expression of their awareness of the field—is followed by a moment of mutual sharing in which each acknowledges the other's subjective experience.[6]

A Side Note. The distinction between deliberate work on the relationship and spontaneous therapeutic activity can help clarify a minor controversy I witnessed during a clinical-educational seminar with Daniel Stern held in Palermo in 2009.[7] On that occasion, Stern stated that it is not always useful to put into words the experience of the encounter between therapist and patient. Commenting with the patient on what happens during key moments of the therapeutic relationship, he said, may be unnecessary or even counterproductive. This observation caused some perplexity among the attendees, most of whom were Gestalt therapists. Some objected, arguing that for Gestalt therapists, it is perfectly normal to talk about what happens in the here and now of the therapeutic relationship. It seemed there was an incomprehensible divergence between Stern's approach and ours.

However, the issue becomes clearer in light of the distinction between deliberate and spontaneous activity. Talking about what happens between patient and therapist, as we Gestalt therapists commonly do, constitutes a valuable technical tool for exploring the relationship. Conversely, such an intervention may become unnecessary or counterproductive in spontaneous activity, as introducing technique into a spontaneous process risks compromising its authenticity. Attempting to explain spontaneity always carries the risk of stifling it.

4.5.2 *The Co-Created Spontaneous Encounter*

In the context of contemporary Gestalt therapy, there is a growing tendency to view what we define here as *spontaneous therapeutic activity* as a key element of change. Healing, therefore, is configured as a real, spontaneous, and co-created encounter between two human beings who fully engage with one another (Spagnuolo Lobb, 2003, 2013). This represents a shift from a technical conception of care to the idea that change depends on the quality of the relationship and the ability to be with the other.[8]

Spontaneous therapeutic activity is made up of moments. According to Daniel Stern and his colleagues at the Boston Change Process Study Group (2010), change occurs not only in moments of intense emotional sharing, known as *moments of meeting*, but also in more subtle, quiet, and seemingly ordinary moments. In both cases, what they have in common is the recognition of the other's subjective reality. These moments of mutual recognition cannot result from any technique or procedure; they occur only when the therapist is fully present in the encounter with the other and expresses themselves and their experience spontaneously.

Similarly, Perls *et al.* (1994, p. 246) argue that spontaneity does not stem directly from technical interventions: "The final stage of the experience is not a subject of therapy." This statement highlights how, for the authors of *Gestalt Therapy*, spontaneous experience, which characterizes the final stage of the contact process, cannot be planned or directly induced. The spontaneity of the process can only be indirectly restored by working on the ego—the system of identifications and alienations—through techniques and experiments aimed at developing awareness. However, in the foundational text of Gestalt therapy, there are references to the spontaneity of the encounter between patient and therapist as a factor of therapeutic change. For example, the following passage highlights the therapist's active involvement, where spontaneity is reflected in their ability to respond authentically and appropriately, based on the "truth of the situation" rather than relying on pre-established techniques or responses:

> The therapist, according to his own self-awareness, declines to be bored, intimidated, cajoled, etc.; he meets anger with explanation of the misunderstanding, or sometimes apology, or even with anger, according to the truth of the situation; he meets obstruction with impatience in the framework of a longer patience. In this way the unaware can become foreground, so that its structure can be experienced.
>
> (Perls *et al.*, 1994, pp. 25–26)

This involvement highlights the spontaneous and co-created nature of the therapeutic encounter, which generates change and growth not only in the patient but also in the therapist. The latter, in fact, "is himself growing into a real situation by giving in to what is brought in and defending himself against the neurotic elements in it" (Perls *et al.*, 1994, pp. 60–61).

The conceptual framework of Gestalt for spontaneous therapeutic activity can be derived from the self theory of Perls, Hefferline, and Goodman, centered on the concept of the spontaneous self. As discussed in previous chapters, spontaneity is an intrinsic quality of the experience of full awareness. We are spontaneous when we are fully present in the here and now. On this point, Perls *et al.* (1994, p. 7) write: "Spontaneity is the seizing on, and glowing and growing with, what is interesting and nourishing in the environment." This state of spontaneity, according to the authors, is characterized by a sense of flowing with the environment in a continuous process of growth.

The spontaneous encounter between two human beings, therefore, represents a reciprocal "seizing" and "being seized" at the same time, where each illuminates the other, and both are transformed together. As the authors state: "They discover themselves and one another and invent themselves and one another" (Perls *et al.*, 1994, p. 87). This process of co-creation and mutual transformation lies at the heart of spontaneous therapeutic activity, which is expressed in the full engagement of both therapist and patient in the shared experience.

According to Perls, Hefferline, and Goodman, spontaneous experience is characterized by the feeling of neither exclusively being the agent of action nor passively undergoing it, but simultaneously acting and being acted upon, as if the action were developing on its own. Spontaneous action, therefore, cannot be classified as exclusively active or passive but exists in a "middle mode." In the spontaneous experience, one is fully engaged, and the sense of self as a separate entity may diminish, giving way to a perception of integration with the ongoing process. Finally, spontaneous action is not oriented toward a pre-established goal or objective but finds its orientation in the very moment of its development.

The properties of spontaneous experience highlighted by Perls, Hefferline, and Goodman find an interesting parallel in Hans-Georg Gadamer's description of the characteristics of play. A leading figure in philosophical hermeneutics, Gadamer (1989) proposed the concept of "play" as a metaphor for our relationship with the world. According to Gadamer, play is structurally analogous to dialogue and encounters with others—moments in which we not only participate but are transformed. A central element of his reflection is the primacy of play over the players: play has its own essence, and those who play are taken by it; they neither create nor control it. In playing, the subject is simultaneously active and passive: "The primordial sense of playing is the medial one" (Gadamer, 1989, p. 103). In other words, play develops in a middle way, where action is neither purely active nor simply passive but a synthesis of both. Immersed in play, the players do not possess a subjectivity that exists independently of the act of playing. As Gadamer states: "The real subject of the game is not the player but instead the game itself" (Gadamer, 1989, p. 106). Furthermore, play has no external purpose other than its self-representation—that is, its manifestation of itself. From this perspective, Gadamer describes play as an open and spontaneous event, of "middle mode," which transcends the individual subjectivity of the players involved. This makes it particularly akin to the spontaneous Gestalt experience, which is also characterized by full engagement and the co-creation of the present moment, in which the self is not lost but dynamically integrates into the process.

For both Perls, Hefferline, and Goodman, and Gadamer, spontaneous encounter and authentic dialogue are not planned or controlled by the interlocutors; rather, they emerge as a process unfolding through them. It is not a deliberate product but an event realized in the here and now. When the therapist is fully present at the contact-boundary, they do not know in advance what the patient's next step will be, nor their own, because "in spontaneous behavior, everything is novel and progressively made one's own" (Perls *et al.*, 1994, p. 161). Only by accepting the risk of facing the unknown—an intrinsic element of living fully in the present—and trusting the self-regulation of the process and the spontaneity of what occurs moment by moment in the encounter with the other, is it possible to open up to the new and grow together.

4.6 The Holistic Approach of Gestalt Therapy

Deliberate and spontaneous therapeutic activities involve different perspectives and ways of engaging in the relationship. This raises a fundamental question: how are these two dimensions of therapeutic action brought together?

Danilo Cargnello, who was the father of phenomenological psychopathology in Italy, in his main work *Alterità e alienità* (2010), distinguishes two opposing clinical attitudes: the naturalistic attitude of "distant objectification" (of which psychoanalysis is a sui generis example) and the intersubjective attitude of "interhuman approach," characteristic of the phenomenological-existential orientation in psychiatry. The naturalistic attitude, based on the separation between the individual and the environment, objectifies the human being, considering him as one of the many objects in the world. The intersubjective attitude, which emphasizes the need to investigate the individual–environment unity, believes that human reality can only be grasped through the interhuman encounter. Although these two fundamental attitudes are essentially antinomical and incommensurable, they are, according to Cargnello, both necessary. The naturalistic approach provides us with a unified, coherent, and systematic method for studying human experience, paving the way for intersubjective understanding. On the other hand, the intersubjective approach, by recognizing the limits of any objectification of the subject, allows us to deepen the knowledge gained from the naturalistic investigation through the analysis of the different ways in which presence unfolds. Psychotherapy, then, according to Cargnello, is a complex process, in which the therapist seamlessly oscillates from one attitude to another, from one plane to another, transferring knowledge elements and aspects of understanding from one to the other.

Deliberate therapeutic activity, in which the therapist observes the process from the outside, distancing themselves, and spontaneous activity, in which the therapist is fully involved, respectively recall the naturalistic objectifying attitude and the intersubjective attitude described by Cargnello. But the Gestalt perspective, which aims to preserve the integrity of reality, allows for overcoming the dichotomy between the two attitudes indicated by Cargnello, which are only seemingly irreconcilable, and fosters an integrated and unified view of the therapeutic process. Deliberate activity and spontaneous activity are inextricably linked in the present situation, they go hand in hand and complement each other. The therapist's theoretical and methodological knowledge helps guide their spontaneous action. On the other hand, focusing on the contact-boundary allows them to better understand what is happening in the specific situation of the moment and, if necessary, to question their clinical reference model.

Perls *et al.* (1994, p. 228) warn: "The therapist needs his conception in order to keep his bearing, to know in what direction to look." However, his prior knowledge must not prevail over the specificity of the present moment, nor prevent him from recognizing the novelty of the current situation, which is always unique and unrepeatable. The therapist does not impose their model of health, their idea of what is healthy and what is not, nor their therapeutic method on the patient; rather, they use them in a flexible and adaptable manner, aware that there is no rule that applies universally. Furthermore, the therapist is always emotionally available and ready to personally engage in the present situation, trusting the spontaneity of the process.

Deliberate and spontaneous therapeutic activities go hand in hand. In healthy experience, deliberate activity, by serving creative adjustment, paves the way for spontaneity. The risk we face, both in therapy and in life, is that the hegemony of the deliberate mode, typical of our neurotic society, may stifle spontaneity. But spontaneity is central to mental health, and spontaneous therapeutic activity constitutes the core of therapeutic change. Simone Weil (2009, p. 193) writes: "The weeds are pulled up by the muscular effort of the peasant, but only sun and water can make the corn grow."

Gestalt therapy is a holistic and integrated approach, which includes both individual work and relational work, both technical approaches and the spontaneous, co-created encounter. Renouncing any of these components, all of which are somehow present in its foundational text, would mean weakening both the theory and practice of Gestalt. Some fundamental concepts of Gestalt therapy, which 70 years ago constituted an original contribution to the psychological clinic of that time, are today a consolidated part of other approaches, which in some cases have perhaps been able to spread them more effectively than Gestalt therapists themselves. Consider, for example, the focus on awareness, which characterizes mindfulness, or the centrality that relational/intersubjective psychoanalysis assigns to the therapeutic relationship and encounter. Today, the specificity of Gestalt therapy does not lie so much in the originality of its epistemological premises or theoretical constructs, but in the way it translates them into therapeutic action. Its global perspective, which integrates the importance of the present moment, the phenomenological work on individual experience, the work on the body, the analysis of the therapeutic relationship, and the spontaneous, co-created encounter, considers all these factors as different dimensions of the unified functioning of the organism/environment field. This still makes Gestalt therapy one of the most valid and current psychotherapeutic approaches.

Notes

1 This chapter is a slightly modified version of the article already published in *Quaderni di Gestalt*, 2018, XXXI, 1: 33–57. https://doi.org/10.3280/GEST2015-002004, and in the *British Gestalt Journal*, 2020, 29, 1: 30–36, which I thank for granting permission for its publication.

2 Already in the lecture delivered in 1947 at the White Institute in New York, Perls (1979) addresses the issue of the split between deliberateness and spontaneity that characterizes modern personality. On that occasion, he distinguishes between two different therapeutic attitudes: one deliberate, which interferes with the biological formation of the figure–ground relationship, and one spontaneous, which instead facilitates it. The first attitude reduces awareness and self-expression, while the second promotes them.

Perls focuses on describing the spontaneous functioning of the organism, highlighting its importance. However, he adds that deliberate activity also plays a fundamental role, provided it is harmoniously placed at the service of the organism's survival and well-being.

3 In this context, I use the term *technique* in a broad sense, to refer to an operational modality mediated by clinical reflection and informed by a theoretical model. In Gestalt psychotherapy—particularly as articulated in *Gestalt Therapy* (Perls *et al.*, 1994)—there is no set of codified techniques to be applied rigidly. Therapeutic intervention does not follow fixed protocols, but is instead constructed moment by moment through a creative adaptation to the patient's current situation and to the quality of the therapeutic relationship. In this sense, therapy is situational, process-oriented, and relational, rather than procedural.

4 This idea is connected to Beisser's *paradoxical theory of change* (1971), which states that an individual changes not when they try to become different from what they are, but when they fully accept themselves as they are. Accepting oneself means focusing attention on what one is experiencing in the present moment, fully feeling it, and taking responsibility for it—recognizing it as one's own and identifying with it. Complementarily, we can affirm that focusing on one's experience fosters its acceptance. Today, thanks to studies on trauma, we know that traumatic experiences impair the self's ability to function spontaneously and integratively. This leads us to reconsider the Gestalt conception of the change process in light of recent neuroscientific discoveries, which highlight the crucial role of brain processes in mediating interactions between the individual and the environment (Taylor, 2014). These discoveries broaden the Gestalt understanding of change by integrating the importance of the body and neural responses in the therapeutic process.

5 Here, I refer to the two domains of experience that Stern (2004) defines as *explicit knowledge* and *implicit knowing*. The former is symbolic, declarative, conscious, verbalizable, and narratable. The latter is non-symbolic, non-verbal, procedural, and non-conscious (in the sense that it is not associated with reflective awareness). Stern views the explicit and implicit dimensions of knowing and memory as two interdependent but distinct domains. Although intentional and spontaneous therapeutic activity can, in many respects, be associated with Stern's two domains, it is important to understand them not as separate aspects of the clinical situation but as different modalities of it. These modalities integrate with one another and cannot be considered independently.

6 I drew inspiration for this example from a passage in *Gestalt Therapy*, which I cite later (see Perls *et al.*, 1994, pp. 25–26).

7 Clinical-Educational Seminar with Daniel Stern: "*Key Moments in Psychotherapy: Embodied Empathy and Intentional Concordance Between Development and Therapy*", held from January 23 to 25, 2009, in Palermo, at the Gestalt Institute HCC Italy, School of Specialization in Gestalt therapy.

8 Recently, Spagnuolo Lobb (2016, 2020) proposed an interpretation of the co-creation of contact between caregiver and child in terms of *dance steps*, understood as modes through which the field self-regulates. This perspective introduces new concepts and terms to describe, from a Gestalt viewpoint, both primary relationships and the therapeutic encounter.

References

Beisser A. (1971). The paradoxical theory of change. In J. Fagan, & I. Shepherd (Eds.), *Gestalt therapy now*. New York, NY: Harper Colophon Books.

Boston Change Process Study Group. (2010). *Change in psychotherapy: A unifying paradigm*. New York, NY: W.W. Norton & Company.

Buber, M. (1958). *I and thou* (R. G. Smith, Trans.). New York, NY: Scribner.

Cargnello, D. (2010). *Alterità e alienità*. Roma: Giovanni Fioriti Editore.

Frank, R. (2001). *Body of awareness: A somatic and developmental approach to psychotherapy*. Highland, NY: Gestalt Press.

Gadamer, H. G. (1989). *Truth and method* (2nd revised ed.). New York, NY: Crossroad. (Original work published 1960 as *Wahrheit und Methode*, Tübingen: J.C.B. Mohr).

Kepner, J. I. (1993). *Body process: Working with the body in psychotherapy*. San Francisco, CA: Jossey-Bass.

Macaluso, M. A. (2020). Deliberateness and spontaneity in Gestalt therapy practice. *British Gestalt Journal*, 29(1), 30–36. (Original work published 2018 as Intenzionalità e spontaneità nell'azione terapeutica gestaltica. *Quaderni di Gestalt*, 31(1), 33–57. https://doi.org/10.3280/GEST2018-001004).

Perls, F. (1969). *Ego, hunger and aggression: The beginning of Gestalt therapy*. New York: Vintage Books (Random House). (Original work published 1947).

Perls, F. (1979). Planned psychotherapy. *Gestalt Journal*, 2(2), 13–25.

Perls, F., Hefferline, R., & Goodman, P. (1951/1994). *Gestalt therapy: Excitement and growth in the human personality*. Highland, NY: The Gestalt Journal Press.

Spagnuolo Lobb, M. (2003). Therapeutic meeting as improvisational co-creation. In M. Spagnuolo Lobb & N. Amendt-Lyon (Eds.), *Creative license: The art of Gestalt therapy* (pp. 37–49). Wien/New York, NY: Springer.

Spagnuolo Lobb, M. (2013). *The now-for-next in psychotherapy: Gestalt therapy recounted in post-modern society*. Milano: FrancoAngeli. (Original work published 2011 as *Il now-for-next in psicoterapia*. Milano: FrancoAngeli).

Spagnuolo Lobb, M. (2016). Gestalt therapy with children: Supporting the polyphonic development of domains in a field of contacts. In M. Spagnuolo Lobb, N. Levi, & A. Williams (Eds.), *Gestalt therapy with children: From epistemology to clinical practice* (pp. 25–62). Siracusa: Istituto di Gestalt HCC Italy Publ. Co.

Spagnuolo Lobb, M. (2020). Dalla perdita delle funzioni-io ai "passi di danza" tra psicoterapeuta e paziente. Fenomenologia ed estetica del contatto nel campo psicoterapeutico. *Quaderni di Gestalt*, 23(1), 21–40. https://doi.org/10.3280/GEST2020-001003

Stern, D. N. (2004). *The present moment in psychotherapy and everyday life*. New York, NY: W. W. Norton & Company.

Taylor, M. (2014). *Trauma therapy and clinical practice: Neuroscience, Gestalt and the body*. Maidenhead: Open University Press.

Weil, S. (2009). *Waiting for god.* New York, NY: Harper Perennial. (Original work published 1950 as *L'attente de Dieu.* Paris: La Colombe).

Wheeler, G. (1991). *Gestalt reconsidered: A new approach to contact and resistance.* New York, NY: Gardner Press.

Yontef, G. (2002). The relational attitude in Gestalt therapy, theory and practice. *International Gestalt Journal*, 25(1), 15–34.

Chapter 5

The Id in Gestalt Therapy[1]

In the theoretical model of Gestalt therapy, the *Id* does not represent, as it does in psychoanalysis, the unconscious dimension of the psyche. On the contrary, the Gestalt id refers to the functioning of the self in states of relaxation and non-integration.

In the previous chapter, I explored the role of intentionality and spontaneity in the Gestalt therapeutic process. The functioning of the self in states of relaxation and non-integration also holds crucial importance in clinical practice. Several authors have analyzed the concept of id in detail, delving into the three modes of partial functioning of the self: Müller (1993), Robine (2004), Spagnuolo Lobb (2013), Macaluso (2015), Wheeler (2016), among others.

In this chapter, I will illustrate how the concept of id represents a fundamental theoretical foundation in contemporary Gestalt therapy, which is relationally oriented. First, I will examine the id both as a phase of the contact process and as one of its modalities. Then, I will focus on the clinical application of the id, analyzing both the role of the patient's id, essential for the integration of experience, and the therapist's id, used as a tool for field awareness.

Furthermore, I will delve into some relational implications of the id in the clinical setting, including intimate sharing between patient and therapist and the practice of joint meditation. Finally, I will highlight how this sharing, occurring at the level of the id, can open up a spiritual dimension, thereby broadening the horizons of therapeutic work.

5.1 The Id as a Phase of the Contact Process

In the previous chapters, we have seen how Perls *et al.* (1994) offer a phenomenological reinterpretation of the psychoanalytic concept of the id, as well as those of the Ego and personality, linking all these elements to the contact process. The authors of *Gestalt Therapy* consider the id—often written with a lowercase initial in their reinterpretation—both as a phase of the contact process and as one of the modalities through which it takes place.[2]

In Gestalt therapy, the contact process unfolds in several stages, from the initial perception of a need or stimulus to its fulfillment through contact with the environment. In this context, the id is described as "the given background dissolving into

DOI: 10.4324/9781003726753-6

its possibilities" (Perls *et al.*, 1994, p. 156). It represents the initial phase of the contact process, the moment when signals of excitement, needs, or desires emerge from the background of awareness. These signals, still vague and lacking a clear form or precise organization, constitute the starting point of the contact process. It is at this stage that awareness begins to organize itself around an emerging new figure.

The id is not simply the unconscious background but the dynamic process through which bodily impulses and sensations emerge in the here and now, involving both the organism and the environment. For example, a vague sensation of hunger (id phase) may evolve into a clearer desire to eat a specific food through interaction with the environment, within the figure/ground process that brings the need into awareness.

Unlike psychoanalysis, which conceptualizes the id as a structural entity separate from consciousness and housing unconscious drives, Gestalt therapy interprets it as a specific mode of the self's functioning, characteristic of the initial phase of the contact process.

5.2 The Id as a Mode of the Contact Process

The id is not merely a transitory phase of the contact process. Under certain circumstances, this phase can stabilize temporarily, becoming a more lasting mode of the self's functioning. This mode emerges when an individual finds themselves in a state of relaxation, where, less influenced by rational control or predefined patterns, the figure/background process develops spontaneously, allowing the experience to manifest fluidly and without interference. As early as *Ego, Hunger and Aggression* (1947/1969), Perls highlights the connection between relaxation and the emergence of figure into awareness. He writes: "In a state of complete relaxation the figure-background formation takes care of itself" (Perls, 1947/1969, p. 230). A little further, he adds: "Let go and get unconcentrated even to the degree of indulging in free associations" (Perls, 1947/1969, p. 231). This state of relaxation and surrender facilitates the spontaneous emergence of a new figure and, consequently, aids in free associations.

In *Gestalt Therapy*, Perls *et al.* (1994, p. 19) define the id as "an extreme of relaxation and loose association," contrasted with the deliberative ego, which represents the other extreme. The id is the least structured dimension of the self, associated with spontaneous and free impulses, while the ego manifests as the more organized and rational dimension. Between these two extremes lies spontaneity, representing the self's ability to creatively and adaptively respond to the needs of the moment, integrating relaxation and deliberation.

To clarify the concept of the id, Perls, Hefferline, and Goodman describe the functioning of the self in a common relaxation situation, such as the state just before sleep. In his first book (Perls, 1947/1969), referring to the ability of visualization, Perls speaks of a "*jumble of meaningless pictures*" that we sometimes experience when we are about to fall asleep. The authors of *Gestalt Therapy* also refer to this particular type of experience to describe the characteristics of the id. In the drowsy phase, they write, the self appears passive, disorganized, and irrational. The contents of awareness seem senseless and mysterious. The excitations that emerge manifest as fleeting impressions, passively experienced and quickly forgotten. The images, of a hallucinatory nature, reflect weak unfinished situations of the day, which release their energy through agitation of the contact-boundary. In this condition, as the self dissolves, the body assumes a central role, as the loosening of control allows repressed proprioceptions to surface into awareness. If these are not strong enough to capture attention, the individual falls asleep.

As Perls *et al.* (1994, p. 160) write: "Relaxation is disintegration, unified only by the looming sense of the body." During relaxation, the body becomes the unifying element, ensuring the continuity of the self even in a state of deconstruction.[3]

In a later passage, the authors return to describe the experience that emerges when we loosen control and let go:

> Under conditions of relaxation, such as free-association or dozing, or again under conditions of spontaneous concentration, such as art-working or lively conversation, at once all kinds of strange images, ideas, abortive impulses and gestures, restless aches and twinges, come to awareness and claim attention: the suppressed excitation that want to develop; and if by disinterested but directed concentration they are given language and muscular means, they immediately reveal themselves with full significance. Such tendencies are, of course, the bread-and-butter of any analytic session; how is it possible that Freud did not assign them weight as evidence for the irrepressibility of id?
>
> (Perls *et al.*, 1994, p. 214)

Relaxation allows spontaneous interests and repressed excitations to emerge and become figure. "Disinterested concentration," a form of open, receptive attention without an immediate goal, allows the expression and development of these unconscious contents, giving rise to a flow of awareness valuable for psychotherapy. This process, the authors of *Gestalt Therapy* conclude, demonstrates that the id cannot be repressed, contrary to what Freud claimed.

In the Gestalt perspective, the id is the disintegrated or unintegrated self, a spontaneous and irrational mode of functioning that manifests during relaxation, when the rational control of the ego diminishes. According to Perls, Hefferline, and Goodman, this lack of integration of the self is not at all a dysfunctional or pathological condition:

> You do not fall apart, go to pieces, or act crazy, if you let up on your deliberate holding back, forcing attention, constant thinking and active interference with the trends of your behavior. Instead, your experience begins to cohere and to organize into more meaningful wholes. [...] When you relinquish your determination to make your behavior fit the arbitrary, more or less fixed pattern that you have taken over from "the authorities", aware need and spontaneous interest

> come to the surface and reveal to you what you are and what it is appropriate for you to do. This is your nature, the very core of your vitality.
>
> (Perls *et al.*, 1994, pp. 358–359)

Suspending deliberate control and surrendering to non-integration, according to the authors of *Gestalt Therapy*, makes it possible to access our integrative potential and inner wisdom. This relaxation allows the self to reorganize in a more authentic way, enabling deep needs and impulses to emerge as figures in the present context.[4]

The id represents the creative dimension of the self, connected to imagination, intuition, and the emergence of new ideas. This dimension is particularly familiar to artists, who learn to exercise a form of unfocused attention to find inspiration. A significant example of the relationship between the artist and the id is provided by the English writer Antonia S. Byatt (2010), who describes the creative process needed to imagine the dreams of her characters:

> I discovered that I can invent dreams for my characters if I immerse myself in a state of absolute vacancy, without observing anything through their eyes. This kind of attention, devoid of specific concentration but intense, has a peculiar relationship with the dreamlike imagination and can generate unreal dreams.
>
> (Byatt, 2010, p. 43)

The id can manifest as the emergence of a new figure, like a sudden insight, or as a spontaneous flow of associations that facilitates the integration of experience and stimulates creativity. Paradoxically, it is precisely the non-integrated functioning of the self that facilitates this integrative flow. Perls, Hefferline, and Goodman distinguish this from Freudian free associations, which tend to turn into a flight of ideas and dispersive digressions, often losing contact with the reality of the present moment and fostering dissociation rather than integration. Moreover, free associations present an additional limitation: they focus primarily on the cognitive dimension of experience (thoughts and images), neglecting bodily, sensory, and emotional aspects.

To overcome these limitations, Perls, Hefferline, and Goodman propose an alternative phenomenological practice, which consists of paying attention to each experience, moment by moment, and verbalizing it by repeating "Now I am aware...". This practice, which Perls would later define as the "continuum of awareness," involves all dimensions of human experience—thoughts, images, sensations, and emotions—integrating them into a harmonious and unified flow.

Unlike mere verbalization without real active involvement, where one passively follows the flow of words, the id is an active and dynamic process. It is not limited to a mental or intrapsychic activity but involves the entire organism in its relationship with the environment. It is a flow of awareness that emerges when we relax, let go of tensions, and focus our attention in an open and flexible way on present reality.

In therapy, therefore, the id is supported by two closely connected conditions. On the one hand, relaxation, in which the self temporarily "disintegrates"—that is, operates in a mode of non-integration—allowing for total openness to experience. On the other hand, disinterested concentration, which enables the observation of the present moment without judgment or interference. The integration of these two elements facilitates a more authentic contact with the environment and with oneself, freeing experience from rigid patterns and allowing for a deeper and more spontaneous transformation.

From this perspective, non-integration is not a problem to be solved but a fertile ground of possibilities, where the self can reorganize in a more creative and authentic way. Therefore, the therapist's role is not to rigidly guide the process but to create the conditions for organismic self-regulation to express itself freely. It is within this space of suspension and openness that change finds its most authentic expression—not as something imposed, but as a natural process of growth and transformation.

5.3 The Unconscious in Gestalt: A Dynamic Background for Conscious Experience

Perls, Hefferline, and Goodman reject Freud's idea of the id as an unconscious reservoir of impulses to be repressed, instead proposing a dynamic approach in which the id and the ego are fluid and interconnected processes that work together to foster creative adjustment. In this perspective, the unconscious is not a separate and inaccessible entity but rather a dynamic resource that actively interacts with the self.

In Gestalt therapy, there is no rigid separation between the conscious and the unconscious. Unconscious contents are seen as a background that can become figure when the individual is ready to become aware of them. The authors of *Gestalt Therapy* argue that repressed desires do not disappear but instead emerge spontaneously when the individual relaxes or focuses, as happens in free associations or creative activities. These impulses, if recognized, can be expressed and expand awareness.

Moreover, the unconscious is not merely a repository of impulses but an integral part of experience and the process of contact with reality. It provides spontaneous and creative responses to new situations and, if not inhibited, fosters a positive adaptation to the environment, supporting the individual in facing present challenges.

5.4 The Id as Field Knowledge

As we have seen previously, when the self operates in the id mode, body awareness is amplified. Perls, Hefferline, and Goodman explain that, in a state of deep relaxation, the self harmonizes with the environment, and the body becomes particularly sensitive to its stimuli. In this regard, they write:

> Now there is a relaxation: the beautiful experience of aesthetic-erotic absorption, when the spontaneous awareness and muscularity drinks in and dances in

> the environment as if self-oblivious, but in fact feeling the deeper parts of the self responding to heightened meaning of the object.
>
> (Perls *et al.*, 1994, p. 37)

This passage describes a state of relaxation in which the individual momentarily seems to forget themselves but actually experiences a deeper connection with their own experience. In this condition, body and mind harmonize with the environment, responding spontaneously and fluidly to external stimuli. Relaxation thus fosters an authentic connection with the body, which becomes the primary mediator between the self and external reality.

When the therapist relaxes and engages in disinterested concentration on what happens at the contact-boundary, the rational mind steps aside, allowing the body to become a sensitive vehicle for perceiving what is occurring in the field. According to Spagnuolo Lobb (2013), the id precisely consists of coming into contact with the environment through bodily sensations. The same author has proposed the concept of *aesthetic relational knowledge* as a way of knowing the field through the senses. Spagnuolo Lobb (2018, p. 64) writes: "The therapist's feeling [...] is not only empathy, identifying with the patient's experience, but it is also resonance, the personal and sensitive reaction to the field in front of the patient." While empathy allows the therapist to understand the patient's lived experience in facing life's difficulties, resonance captures the reaction of the significant other—the "other side of the moon" of the patient's experience. By focusing on bodily sensations, the therapist can grasp the patient's experiential background and support them in completing their interrupted contact intentionality. The body thus becomes the primary tool that enables the therapist to navigate the clinical situation.

Aesthetic relational knowledge, which arises from surrendering to the stream of sensations and impressions co-created at the contact-boundary and mediated by cognitive empathy (Spagnuolo Lobb *et al.*, 2023), is a form of knowledge that expresses the integration of the self's functioning. Although it is based on bodily sensations, it is also a type of intuitive knowledge.

Intuition, writes Perls (1947/1969, p. 212), is "harmony of thinking and being", a form of direct knowledge that results from the integration of cognition, sensation, and emotion. According to Perls, Hefferline, and Goodman, intuition is a kind of "hallucination", through which we grasp what has not yet fully manifested, what we only vaguely sense: "By intuition or prescience we are warned of or invited by the meaning not yet apparent" (Perls *et al.*, 1994, p. 234). Intuition allows us to go beyond the surface and "see" deeply into ourselves and the world. A recent study by Spagnuolo Lobb *et al.* (2023) demonstrates that *aesthetic relational knowledge* is a multidimensional construct that includes empathy, resonance, and bodily awareness.

For the therapist, aesthetic relational knowledge is the counterpart of the continuum of awareness for the patient. Both of these Gestalt clinical tools involve a state of relaxation and disinterested concentration, open to all stimuli. Both are based on the same process—the id—but are experienced from different positions and with different purposes. The continuum of awareness facilitates the patient's processing and integration of experiences, while aesthetic relational knowledge enables the therapist to perceive what is happening moment by moment in the field. We could say that, in Gestalt therapy, the continuum of awareness relates to aesthetic relational knowledge in the same way that, in psychoanalysis, free association relates to floating attention.

In his 1912 paper, "Recommendations to Physicians Practising Psycho-Analysis," Freud (1958, pp. 111–112) states that the psychoanalyst's first practical rule, which summarizes all the others, "consists simply in not directing one's notice to anything in particular and in maintaining the same 'evenly-suspended attention' (as I have called it) in the face of all one hears." Freud warns that by deliberately focusing one's attention, one inevitably ends up selecting the material based on one's own inclinations or expectations. The psychoanalyst should, however, beware of privileging any material, considering all information on an equal footing. They should therefore maintain an evenly-suspended attention—one that is diffuse and not centered on any particular element.

Despite our usual tendency to presuppose and plan, Freud (1958, p. 114) states that in psychoanalytic treatment,

> the most successful cases are those in which one proceeds, as it were, without any purpose in view, allows oneself to be taken by surprise by any new turn in them, and always meets them with an open mind, free from any presuppositions.

The most valuable insights and therapeutic interventions emerge from an attitude of receptiveness and openness to novelty and unpredictability.

Freud's specific recommendations on evenly-suspended attention have often been overlooked by psychoanalysts, likely because it is difficult to suspend our habitual rational control. According to Epstein (2007), the decline in trust in evenly-suspended attention has deprived psychoanalysis of one of its most powerful tools.

The evenly-suspended attention described by Freud and the aesthetic relational knowledge proposed by Spagnuolo Lobb are two fundamentally different receptive dispositions. The former pertains primarily to the cognitive level of experience and, as Perls, Hefferline, and Goodman state, can easily lead to a dispersive flight of ideas. The latter, on the other hand, is primarily based on sensory data and connection with the present moment. Despite their differences, these two important clinical tools rely on the same spontaneous process, not guided by deliberateness, free from ego control, and open to everything that emerges—what Perls, Hefferline, and Goodman call the id.

5.5 Other Receptive Dispositions Related to the Id

Perls adopted the concepts of *zero point* and *creative indifference* from the philosopher Salomo Friedlaender (Frambach, 2003). The *zero point* is the intermediate point between the two opposites of a continuum. It represents a position of *indifference*, or *disinterest*, which allows for a broader and less distorted view of reality.[5] *Creative indifference* consists in being "uncommittedly interested in the opposites" (Perls *et al.*, 1994, p. 294). *Creative indifference* does not imply a neutral stance between opposites but rather a total openness to embracing all possibilities, fully responding to the reality of the moment.

The state of openness and availability inherent in *creative indifference* recalls the experience of *internal silence*, described by Perls (1947/1969) as "the one way by which we can contact the deeper layers of our existence, rejuvenate our thinking and gain 'intuition'" (p. 212). *Creative indifference* and *inner silence* are analogous to another concept developed by Perls: the *fertile void*, which signifies freeing oneself from any preconception or predetermined perspective, surrendering instead to a generalized openness. The *fertile void* represents the state of openness that allows the self's creativity to emerge spontaneously. It is the dimension that enables change, the original source of the self-therapeutic power inherent in each of us.

The notions of *zero point*, *creative indifference*, *internal silence*, and *fertile void* describe states of openness and receptivity that are based on relaxation and disinterested concentration. In Gestalt therapy, these receptive dispositions, all linked to a single process—the id—represent not only moments of suspension of control but also the fertile ground from which intuition, creativity, and transformation emerge.

5.6 Therapeutic *Non-Action* and Intimate Sharing

The concept of the id allows us to further develop the reflection on the relational orientation in Gestalt therapy, laying the groundwork for the conceptualization of an intimate dimension within the therapeutic relationship.

The therapist's id is not only a way of knowing but also a way of operating. As we have seen, in the id mode of the self, the therapist adopts an attitude of openness and receptivity toward everything that emerges, whether verbal or non-verbal, explicit or implicit, both in the patient and in themselves. In this way, they position themselves at the contact-boundary with a disinterested stance: they are neither active nor entirely passive. Regarding the passivity of the id, Perls *et al.* (1994, p. 159) write: "The sense of passivity comes from the act of accepting without engagement." The passivity of the id should be understood as availability, openness, and acceptance. The therapist's id mode of functioning does not exclude action; rather, it implies it. What, then, are the characteristics of therapeutic action within relaxation and the non-integration of the self? To answer this question, it is useful to refer to the Taoist concept of *non-action* (*wu-wei*).

According to Taoism, the universe is harmony, nature is harmony. Everything self-regulates spontaneously, as long as human action does not disturb the harmony of the Tao, the principle from which all things originate. Hence the concept of *non-action*, which does not literally mean doing nothing but rather refraining from actions that are not in harmony with the natural flow of things. The most effective attitude for achieving one's goals is precisely to allow oneself to be guided by the changing course of events. However, this does not mean being passive or resigned.

On the contrary, it is essential to align with what naturally unfolds. This concept is expressed in the following Chinese maxim: "Do nothing, yet let nothing be left undone." *Non-action* consists of choosing the right actions—those that, by following the spontaneous development of events, gradually lead to the realization of one's objective.

The Taoist principle of *wu-wei* implies an action that follows the natural flow of events, effortlessly and without unnecessary interference. This concept finds a remarkable resonance in Gestalt therapy, which views the organism's self-regulation as a natural process, capable of restoring balance if not hindered by forced interventions. Even in therapy, change emerges spontaneously when space is given to the process rather than attempting to direct it deliberately. This same principle is clearly expressed by the authors of *Gestalt Therapy*:

> It is not necessary deliberately to schedule, to encourage or inhibit, the promptings of appetite, sexuality, and so forth, in the interests of health or morals. If these things are let be, they will spontaneously regulate themselves, and if they have been deranged, they will tend to right themselves. [...] We reiterate that the suggestion is a spectacularly conservative one, for it is nothing but the old advice of the Tao: "stand out of the way".
>
> (Perls *et al.*, 1994, pp. 23–24)

In the id mode of the self, the therapist practices *non-action*: a receptive attention and a total openness to the therapeutic process. They surrender to the flow of events, following the process without attempting to direct it. Nevertheless, they are neither inactive nor ineffective. Their presence influences the development of the field. They remain with the suffering of the other without trying to analyze or explain it. They do not attempt to modify the other's experience or to make them feel better, yet paradoxically, this very stance fosters change. They expect no specific outcome, other than the natural unfolding of growth.[6]

Non-action, as practiced by the therapist when relinquishing rational control and remaining fully open and available, is fundamentally aimed at attuning with the other and unfolds within this attunement. Through this, a deep communication—or rather, an intimate sharing—takes place between patient and therapist, constituting an important therapeutic factor.

This intimacy is not a random occurrence but can be actively cultivated by the therapist through techniques that foster full presence and authentic sharing in the here and now. In Gestalt therapy, specific practices help create the conditions for this transformative experience. The therapist facilitates this dimension through tools such as the continuum of awareness, aesthetic relational knowledge, and the conscious use of silence. All these modalities, rooted in full presence and deep listening, allow the patient to feel genuinely received and understood. In this state of reciprocal openness, the experience of one's id attunes with that of the other, allowing transformation to emerge naturally through the relationship.

French philosopher and sinologist François Jullien (2013) has written an insightful essay on intimacy. He defines intimacy as the space that opens between two people when both, letting go and renouncing their habitual defensive mechanisms, eliminate the boundary that separates their selves. Intimacy means opening to the other, going beyond one's ego. Jullien observes that, etymologically, the term *intimate*—from Latin—has two meanings: on the one hand, it refers to what is most internal and profound within us; on the other, it pertains to the relationship with the other. In intimacy, contact with what is deepest within oneself translates into an opening to the other; and through openness to the other, one deepens contact with one's own inner core. Intimacy is a free experience, with no specific goal. It is fertile, promoting personal growth and transforming one's experience. Since, in intimacy, boundaries dissolve, the experience of the other is grasped not through inference or analogy but immediately, as it unfolds in synchrony with one's own experience.

Jullien considers intimacy in the context of romantic relationships. However, in my view, an intimate sharing also takes place within the therapeutic relationship when both patient and therapist, accepting the risk of stepping outside the safety of their ego, surrender to the non-integrated functioning of the self. The id opens one to the other, immediately creating conditions of intimacy. Each person directly perceives the other's experience and attunes to it. In this situation, one's id exists in relation to the other's id. Rather than communicating something specific, the id unites. And in this intimacy, the self mobilizes and opens to new possibilities. The experience of sharing non-integration enriches the self. By opening to the other through non-integration, the self integrates; and by integrating, it becomes more capable of opening to the other.

This is how we can understand the attunement between one's own unconscious and the patient's unconscious, which Freud (1958) recommended to the psychoanalyst, using a distinctly technical metaphor: "He must turn his own unconscious like a receptive organ toward the transmitting unconscious of the patient. He must adjust himself to the patient as a telephone receiver is adjusted to the transmitting microphone" (p. 115).

The idea of therapy as an experience of intimate emotional sharing finds support in the theories of Allan Schore, an American neuropsychologist who has long worked on integrating psychoanalytic thought with neuroscience. Extending to the therapeutic process the findings of research on infant-caregiver interaction, Schore (2003) asserts that between patient and therapist, an unconscious communication of emotional states occurs through the right hemisphere of one and the right hemisphere of the other—a pre-verbal, implicit dialogue based on somatosensory signals. This immediate emotional communication between right hemispheres, which takes place particularly during emotionally intimate and intense moments through synchronized and reciprocal temporary regressions, plays a crucial role in the therapeutic process. According to Schore, this process enables integration, emotional regulation, and affective growth.

Therapeutic non-action and intimate sharing are not merely attitudes but genuine transformative tools in Gestalt therapy. When the therapist relinquishes rational control and fully opens to the present moment experience, a space of deep connection with the patient is created. In this space, the self resonates with the other, fostering a process of spontaneous self-regulation that leads to growth and integration. Just as Taoism teaches to flow with reality, Gestalt therapy invites the therapist to be fully present, allowing transformation to emerge naturally from the relational field.

5.7 Id, Meditation, and the Spiritual Dimension

Jack Kornfield (1993), a psychologist and meditation teacher who played a key role in the spread of Buddhist practice and psychology in the West, argues that the best of modern psychotherapy resembles a process of shared meditation. In this process, the therapist and patient sit together, learning to direct deep attention to aspects and dimensions of the self that the patient may not be able to contact alone.

The various expressions and designations of the id in Perls' work—such as the zero point, creative indifference, the fertile void, and internal silence—recall some Buddhist meditation practices that emphasize the ability to focus attention and observe the workings of one's mind as a method to access a meditative state characterized by open attention and a lack of attachment to thoughts.[7]

There are numerous points of contact, in particular, between the continuum of awareness practiced in Gestalt therapy and Vipassana, an ancient form of Buddhist meditation based on focusing attention on the lived experience in the present. This practice views the flow of thoughts, sensations, and emotions as elements that spontaneously arise in consciousness moment by moment, without being held onto or rejected.

The continuum of awareness, which Perls introduced even before realizing it was a typical Buddhist meditative technique, can be seen as a form of "loud meditation." Indeed, while in Vipassana the inner experience is observed in silence, in Gestalt the individual is encouraged to verbalize what emerges, bringing awareness and integration into the therapeutic process. In this sense, it can be stated that meditation is not merely a cultural reference for Gestalt, but a dimension that permeates its therapeutic approach.

Claudio Naranjo (1993, 1999) was the first to propose the application of traditional forms of individual meditation, particularly Vipassana, to interpersonal relationships. In the 1960s, he introduced specific two-person meditation exercises, both in Gestalt therapy training courses and in clinical practice. These exercises represent an adaptation of the continuum of awareness technique in a relational key.

In the therapeutic setting, the patient and therapist, sitting across from each other, adopt a meditative attitude, relaxing and paying disinterested attention to what emerges in the here and now, at the contact-boundary. Both remain present to the other's experience and, simultaneously, to their own. After an initial phase of silent meditation, the patient begins to verbalize their experience. The therapist, instead of analyzing or interpreting what is said, welcomes what happens both inside and outside themselves, paying attention to the nuances of the interaction. Occasionally, they intervene with observations, questions, or by sharing an insight.

In this process, the therapist does not seek to direct or control the experience but relies on the spontaneous emergence of the moment. By facing the other, in a state of creative indifference, they allow the relationship to develop freely, exercising a therapeutic action not through explicit interventions but through the quality of their silent presence. Naranjo defines this phenomenon as "contagion of consciousness," meaning the therapist's mindful presence facilitates an expansion of awareness in the patient.

According to Naranjo, the introduction of interpersonal meditation into therapy enhances the effectiveness of clinical work, promoting the integration between the psychotherapeutic experience and the spiritual dimension. In these moments of shared meditation, both the therapist and the patient are invited to transcend the boundaries of their own self, paving the way for more authentic and intimate contact. This approach facilitates a deep connection that transcends usual roles, allowing for a temporary dissolution of defenses and direct interaction with the other's experience.

In Gestalt therapy, the experience of the id helps the patient achieve a state of openness and presence, freeing the self from habitual conditioning and attuning to the flow of experience. This process echoes descriptions of the spiritual dimension, where the abandonment of rational control and identification with the ego leads to a broader and interconnected perception of reality.

By delving into the concept of the id and some of its implications, we enter a territory that is still often little explored: the spiritual or mystical dimension in psychotherapy. This dimension, distinct from religious discourse, essentially concerns the transcendence of the individual, the overcoming of egocentrism. It is through this shedding of the ego that the human being attains a deep and revealing intuition of the unity of all things.

Contact with one's spiritual dimension represents a profound form of self-support, capable of generating inner strength, freedom, and joy. Marco Vannini, in his book *La morte dell'anima. Dalla mistica alla psicologia* (2004), emphasizes how Western culture has separated spirituality from daily life, relegating it to the realm of the supernatural. He argues that, in reality, spirituality is an integral part of human experience and, as such, should be reclaimed in psychotherapeutic practice.

Access to the spiritual dimension in psychotherapy should happen naturally, without force. This is only possible if the therapist has embarked on a personal journey of inner growth. Only then can their presence facilitate authentic experiences for the patient. As Simone Weil writes:

> Only a predestined being has the faculty to ask another: "What is your torment?" And this is not given to him at birth. He must go through years of dark nights, wandering in misfortune, far from everything he loves, with the awareness of his own curse. But in the end, he receives the ability to ask such a

question, and at that very moment, he receives the stone of life and heals the suffering of others.

(Translated from the Italian edition of Weil, Bousquet, 1994, p. 14)

In Gestalt therapy, the therapist does not "teach" the spiritual dimension to the patient, nor does he try to guide them toward a particular transcendental experience. Rather, he facilitates a space of openness and authenticity, where the patient can, spontaneously, come into contact with deeper aspects of the self. The experience of the id, through practices such as the continuum of awareness and interpersonal meditation, creates the conditions for the ego to temporarily dissolve, allowing for a deeper connection with the present moment. In this state of openness, the patient can experience a broader awareness, which not only facilitates the therapeutic process but can also become a fundamental resource for personal growth and inner well-being.

5.8 Conclusions

The concept of the id represents, in my view, a fundamental theoretical premise for the new relational and aesthetic orientation of contemporary Gestalt therapy. The Gestalt therapist oriented toward relationship does not primarily rely on the ego, on the rational and voluntaristic mode of the self, because rationality is not sufficient to understand the emotional experience of the other. This can only be grasped intuitively. Certainly, intuition needs the support of rationality, and a proper integration of the different ways in which the self functions is necessary for the field to develop in a truly transformative way. The therapist, in fact, cannot rely solely on what they feel or on their own intuitions. Furthermore, they cannot freely express their own feelings. However, an over-reliance on rationality hampers the therapeutic process, as it tends to sideline the therapist's feeling and intuition.

Thanks to their aesthetic sensitivity, the therapist perceives aspects of the situation that normally escape attention, as they can be sensed more through the senses than through intellect. Relationally oriented Gestalt therapy values those receptive attitudes connected to the id, which are closer to the body and intuition than to rationality.

In *Gestalt Therapy*, Perls, Hefferline, and Goodman see the id primarily as a tool for integrating the patient's experience. However, the id is also a vehicle for knowledge for the therapist. It constitutes the theoretical foundation of *relational aesthetic knowledge*, described by Spagnuolo Lobb (2018) as a fundamental clinical tool centered on relationship, which allows the therapist to grasp and complete the intentionalities of contact that emerge from the field.

The default state of the Gestalt therapist is the id, characterized by unfocused, open attention. Like a radar, this attention allows one to perceive with sensitivity everything that happens in the field, in the other, and in ourselves. The id enables the therapist to orient themselves and respond to the patient in an appropriate and spontaneous way. Moreover, it fosters a deep connection with the other's experience, creating intimacy and union, and becoming not only a tool for knowledge but also for change.

Finally, the id constitutes the meditative aspect of Gestalt therapy, which introduces us to the spiritual dimension, an integral part of human experience. Including this dimension in the therapeutic process allows us to provide a new horizon for clinical work, going beyond the ego and promoting a broader and more inclusive vision of existence. Eva Gold and Stephen Zahm suggest that psychological growth and spiritual transformation are not separate processes, but part of a unified path of human development. To express our potential, it is essential to address both individual psychological issues and to engage in a practice that helps us understand our existence more deeply—viewing the human path as a continuum rather than a division between psychology and spirituality (Gold & Zahm, 2018).

The aspirations for scientific rigor in psychotherapy, based on the medical model, have led it to neglect the spiritual dimension. But today, in a postmodern world that, in light of quantum physics discoveries, has questioned the universal validity of the foundations of classical science, can we still conceive psychotherapy based on the 19th-century medical model? An important aspect of psychological health is the ability to transcend the ego. This should also be a goal of Gestalt therapy. The id can pave the way for a new model of psychotherapy, one that is aesthetic and intuitive, capable of considering also the deep and transcendent dimension of human experience.

Notes

1 Already published in *Quaderni di Gestalt* (2022), 35(1), 47–67. https://doi.org/10.3280/GEST2022-001004

2 The preference for lowercase reflects the Gestalt view of the self as unified, dynamic, and indivisible into separate parts. Writing *ego* and *id* in lowercase helps convey this fluidity and avoids any interpretation that defines them as rigid entities or places them within a hierarchy.

3 Relaxation amplifies body awareness, but the opposite is also true: focusing attention on bodily sensations promotes relaxation and facilitates the transition of the *self* from the *ego* mode to the *id* mode. This happens because the body becomes the access point to spontaneous and unstructured experiences. Paying attention to the breath or noticing what is happening in the body in the present moment are fundamental starting points in the Gestalt therapeutic process.

4 Winnicott also attributes particular value to relaxation and unintegration. According to Winnicott (1965, p. 61), "*Relaxation for an infant means not feeling a need to integrate, the mother's ego-supportive function being taken for granted.*" He introduces the concept of "unintegration" to describe a state of lack of self-structuring, which is not pathological but rather a natural and necessary condition from which personal creativity can emerge. According to Winnicott, mental health depends not only on the ability to integrate the self but also on the capacity to experience unintegration, a temporary regression that can occur in the presence of a sufficiently good environment.

5 The concept of *zero point* is also present in Søren Kierkegaard, who, in *Either/Or* (1843/1992), describes it as a condition of unstable equilibrium between opposing alternatives, characterized by permanent indecision. However, while for Kierkegaard this state

represents an existential impasse, in Friedlaender and Perls it takes the form of a position of creative openness and receptivity to the reality of the moment.

6 According to Winnicott (1971, pp. 89–90), with some patients and at certain moments, the therapist's task is to tolerate the lack of integration and observe what emerges, without immediately trying to attribute meaning to it. In this way, a particular situation is created in which the therapist remains present with the other without forcing a rational understanding of the experience and without setting a specific goal.

7 For Winnicott (1965), unintegration represents a mode of experience that is close to meditation, which he considers a form of "secret communication with subjective objects."

References

Byatt, A. S. (2010, August 17). Come s'inventa un sogno. *La Repubblica*, p. 43.

Epstein, M. (2007). *Psychotherapy without the self: A Buddhist perspective*. New Haven, CT: Yale University Press.

Frambach, L. (2003). The weighty world of nothingness: Salomo Friedlaender's "creative indifference". In M. Spagnuolo Lobb & N. Amendt-Lyon (Eds.), *Creative license: The art of Gestalt therapy* (pp. 113–127). Wien/New York, NY: Springer.

Freud, S. (1958). Recommendations to physicians practising psycho-analysis. In J. Strachey (Ed. & Trans.), *The standard edition of the complete psychological works of Sigmund Freud* (Vol. 12, pp. 109–120). London: Hogarth Press. (Original work published 1912 as *Ratschläge für den Arzt bei der psychoanalytischen Behandlung*, in *Gesammelte Werke*, Bd. 8, Frankfurt am Main: Fischer, 1999).

Gold, E., & Zahm, S. (2018). *Buddhist psychology & Gestalt therapy integrated*. Portland, OR: Metta Press.

Jullien, F. (2013). *De l'intime: Loin du bruyant amour*. Paris: Grasset & Fasquelle.

Kierkegaard, S. (1992). *Either/or: A fragment of life* (A. Hannay, Trans., Abridged version). London/New York, NY: Penguin. (Original work published 1843 as *Enten-Eller. Et Livs-Fragment, udgivet af Victor Eremita*. Copenhagen: C. A. Reitzel).

Kornfield, J. (1993). *A path with heart: A guide through the perils and promises of spiritual life*. New York, NY: Bantam Books.

Macaluso, M. A. (2015). La teoria del sé in Gestalt Therapy: Il sé, l'Io, l'Es e la personalità. *Quaderni di Gestalt*, 28(2), 61–78. https://doi.org/10.3280/GEST2015-002004

Macaluso, M. A. (2022). L'es in psicoterapia della Gestalt. *Quaderni di Gestalt*, 35(1), 47–67. https://doi.org/10.3280/GEST2022-001004

Müller, B. (1993). Isadore From's contribution to the theory and practice of Gestalt therapy. *Studies in Gestalt Therapy*, 2, 7–21.

Naranjo, C. (1993). *The attitude and practice of Gestalt therapy*. Nevada City, CA: Gateways/IDHHB.

Naranjo, C. (1999). *The way of silence and the way of words: Bringing meditation into psychotherapy* (Republished as *The way of silence and the talking cure: On meditation and psychotherapy*). Nevada City, CA: Blue Dolphin Publishing.

Perls, F. (1969). *Ego, hunger and aggression: The beginning of Gestalt therapy*. New York: Vintage Books (Random House). (Original work published 1947).

Perls, F., Hefferline, R., & Goodman, P. (1951/1994). *Gestalt therapy: Excitement and growth in the human personality*. Highland, NY: The Gestalt Journal Press.

Robine, J.-M. (2004). *Plis et Déplis du Self*. Bordeaux: Institut Français de Gestalt-thérapie. (Original work published 1977).

Schore, A. N. (2003). *Affect regulation and the repair of the self.* New York, NY: W. W. Norton & Company.
Spagnuolo Lobb, M. (2013). *The now-for-next in psychotherapy: Gestalt therapy recounted in post-modern society*. Milano: FrancoAngeli. (Original work published 2011 as *Il now-for-next in psicoterapia*, Milano: FrancoAngeli).
Spagnuolo Lobb, M. (2018). Aesthetic relational knowledge of the field: A revised concept of awareness in Gestalt therapy and contemporary psychiatry. *Gestalt Review*, 22(1), 50–68.
Spagnuolo Lobb, M., Sciacca, F., Iacono Isidoro, S., & Hichy, Z. (2023). A measure for psychotherapist's intuition: Construction, development, and pilot study of the aesthetic relational knowledge scale (ARKS). *The Humanistic Psychologist*, 51(1), 36–55.
Vannini, M. (2004). *La morte dell'anima: Dalla mistica alla psicologia.* Firenze: Le Lettere.
Weil, S., & Bousquet, J. (1994). *Corrispondenza.* Milano: SE. (Original work published 1982 as *Correspondance*. Lausanne: L'Age d'Homme).
Wheeler, G. (2016). The future of the self: Reflections on contact, development, and the "sub-systems of the self" in Paul Goodman. *Gestalt Review*, 20(3), 235–256.
Winnicott, D. W. (1965). *The maturational processes and the facilitating environment: Studies in the theory of emotional development.* London: The Hogarth Press and the Institute of Psycho-analysis.
Winnicott, D. W. (1971). *Playing and reality*. London: Tavistock Publications.

Chapter 6

Rediscovering the Id in Dreamwork

A Gestalt Approach through the Continuum of Awareness[1]

6.1 Introduction

For Gestalt therapy, as for most psychotherapeutic approaches, dreams hold considerable potential for personal transformation, and working with dream material can prove to be a powerful therapeutic tool. The Gestalt approach does not focus on interpreting the unconscious contents of the psyche but on direct experience in the present moment. Therefore, Gestalt work with dreams uses the dream not to decipher a hidden meaning, but as a means to experience something new and transformative. The dream, lived in the here and now, becomes a catalyst for the therapeutic process, whose goal is the spontaneous and integrated functioning of the self.

The two classical methods of Gestalt therapy for working with dreams were developed by Frederick Perls and Isadore From. According to Perls (1969), every element of the dream represents a projection of fragmented parts of the dreamer. The therapist's task is to facilitate the reintegration of these parts, helping the patient to identify with the different elements of the dream.

Alongside this approach, From (Rosenfeld, 1978) proposed considering the dream as a form of retroflection, a mechanism through which the patient repeats to themselves what they have avoided expressing to the therapist during the session. In this perspective, remembering and recounting the dream in therapy becomes an attempt to resolve this retroflection. As a result, From interprets the dream in relational terms, viewing it as a useful tool for bringing to light contact-boundary disturbances in the relationship between patient and therapist. While Perls' approach emphasizes the integration of fragmented parts of the self, From's approach focuses more on the function of the dream within the therapeutic relationship.

In addition to these classical methods, there is another Gestalt approach to working with dreams, used by the Perls couple in the early days of Gestalt therapy and mentioned in the two foundational texts of the discipline. In *Ego, Hunger and Aggression* (Perls, 1947/1969), a concise yet clear technique of dreamwork based on concentration is described. Even in *Gestalt Therapy* (Perls *et al.*, 1951), there

DOI: 10.4324/9781003726753-7

are some brief but significant references to the application of concentration in dreamwork.

Between the 1940s and 1950s, Perls and his wife Laura worked with dreams through concentration in the therapeutic groups they conducted in New York. As Richard Kitzler (2003) recalls, this approach to dream material was initially used in Gestalt clinical practice but was later set aside and gradually forgotten.

Since we do not have a detailed description of the application methods for this technique, nor clinical examples to help fill this gap, I will propose a method of working with dreams through concentration and the continuum of awareness, which I have experimented with in my clinical practice.

The concept of the *id* plays a central role in this approach to dreamwork. As discussed in the previous chapter, Perls, Hefferline, and Goodman define the id as a mode of self-functioning that emerges during relaxation and the suspension of rational control. This state facilitates the emergence of new figures or a spontaneous flow of awareness, promoting the integration of experience. Similarly to what happens in dreams, the non-integration of the id allows the surfacing of images, emotions, and impulses that can facilitate this integration. The proposed technique, based on this mode of functioning, enables the patient to explore and integrate unexpressed experiences.

6.2 The Dream in the Gestalt Approach

Going beyond the Freudian perspective, which sees the dream as wish fulfillment, Perls, Hefferline, and Goodman (1994, p. 38) attribute a broader role to dreams in relation to the spontaneity of the self and the integration of personality. In the first volume of *Gestalt Therapy* (1994, p. 221), the dream is described as a genuine manifestation of the spontaneity of the self, an essential part of an individual's vital reality, and fundamental for any creative operation. It is "concrete, nonverbal, sensory — 'eidetic'" (1994, p. 217), meaning that it expresses itself through vivid images that represent direct sensory experiences rather than abstract concepts or verbalizations. The dream uses a primordial and immediate language, rich in images and emotions, similar to the preverbal language typical of early childhood. This contributes to its apparent incomprehensibility.

In the second volume of the same work (1994, p. 465), the authors present the dream as a projection of the dreamer's current situation, reflecting Perls' classic perspective.[2] Since the dream is a creation of the dreamer, every element represents aspects of their personality and contributes to the construction of the dream itself. By identifying with each element of the dream, the individual can reclaim their split or alienated parts and reintegrate them into their personality. This vision of the dream as a tool for integration is further explored by Perls in *Gestalt Therapy Verbatim* (1969), where he describes the dream as the most spontaneous expression of human existence, uninfluenced by conscious intentions or will. Perls reformulates Sigmund Freud's statement that the dream is the "royal road to the unconscious," instead defining it as the "royal road to integration." This perspective emphasizes how the dream not only reveals unconscious content but also offers the opportunity to reunite fragmented parts of the personality, fostering a process of growth and self-awareness.

In summary, Gestalt therapy assigns a central role to the dream in the therapeutic process, considering it not only as an expression of repressed desires but also as a spontaneous manifestation of the self, reflecting deep aspects of personality and the individual's current state. This approach highlights the importance of dreams as a tool for personality integration, going beyond traditional psychoanalytic interpretations.

6.3 Dreamwork in Early Gestalt Therapy

The dream, therefore, is a spontaneous and creative act of the self and represents an essential resource for therapy, as it is a powerful tool to promote better integration of experience. According to the founders of Gestalt therapy, it should neither be interpreted nor approached through a cold and rational technique, such as free association. They propose, alternatively, to apply the technique of *concentration* to the dream.

Already in *Ego, Hunger and Aggression*, Perls criticizes the use of the free association method for dream analysis, arguing that it fragments the dream and leads more to dissociation than to the integration of experience. Instead, he proposes an approach that allows working with the dream as a whole. This approach, which he calls "chewing," corresponds to his technique of concentration and consists of observing and describing in detail the particulars of the dream to fully assimilate them.

Focusing attention on an aspect of the dream facilitates the change of the initial figure, bringing forth new images or related memories. In this way, integration and closure of unfinished situations are promoted: "The detail description of dream morsels and the blotted out details will bring about their assimilation and understanding" (Perls, 1947/1969, p. 204).

Perls argues that concentration is more effective than free association in promoting awareness and assimilation of the dream, helping to resolve unprocessed situations and facilitating greater integration of lived experience.

In the same vein, the authors of *Gestalt Therapy* criticize free association because it does not help the patient become directly self-aware but keeps them in a passive position, away from an authentic and transformative experience.

They propose considering free association applied to the dream not as an interpretative tool but as an expressive modality that can enrich language and facilitate a deeper connection with lived experience. In their view, the value of free association lies not so much in recovering childhood contents but in reactivating the perceptual and expressive mode of childhood, rediscovering a more immediate, sensory, and emotional way of seeing the world. However, they add: "But from this point of view, the best exercise would perhaps be not free-association from the image and application of cold knowledge to the image, but just the contrary: careful literary and pictorial representation of the it (surrealism)" (Perls *et al.*, 1994, p. 108).

The careful representation that Perls, Hefferline, and Goodman suggest applying to the literary and pictorial aspects of a dream detail can be related to the technique of concentration and the "detailed description" recommended by Perls in *Ego, Hunger and Aggression*, although the latter does not necessarily imply artistic elaboration but rather a process of focusing on details to promote the assimilation of experience.

The method of concentration allows immersion in the language of dream images, rather than reducing them to rational interpretations, and connects ideas, images, and words in a fluid and spontaneous manner, without rigid rational control. In this way, communication between rational (verbal) language and the more primitive and sensory (pre-verbal) language is facilitated, promoting integration between logical thinking and deep emotional experience.

In a later passage (Perls *et al.*, 1994, pp. 216–218), Perls, Hefferline, and Goodman suggest adopting a disinterested concentration—capable of modifying the usual figure/ground formation and altering the backgrounds of the self's reality—in order to facilitate the emergence of the dream and allow it to express itself. In other words, disinterested concentration alters the usual way of organizing perception, allowing elements that are normally relegated to the background—such as dream contents or other excitations—to surface into awareness.

Finally, the testimony of Richard Kitzler (2003) is valuable, recalling how, between the late 1940s and early 1950s, during the founding phase of Gestalt therapy, the Perlses, in therapy groups in their New York studio, worked on dreams through concentration, using the technique initially presented by Perls in *Ego, Hunger and Aggression* and later revisited by Perls, Hefferline, and Goodman in *Gestalt Therapy*. Kitzler (2003) observes regarding this innovative approach to dreams:

> Gestalt therapy stood the relation on its head: it was not the meaning that was crucial, but what the dreamer did with the dream in the session—that is, in the experiment. The emphasis was on the *how* of the dream, the work of it, where it was going (by itself!): its colors or chiaroscuro, movement, sounds, and its novelties. Above all, its novelties, that which had not appeared in the dream itself, but which generated themselves within the structure as it revealed itself.
>
> (p. 102)

This approach highlights the importance of the dreamer's active interaction with their own dream during therapy, privileging the present experience and the emergence of new elements during the exploration of the dream.

In summary, the approach of the founders of Gestalt therapy values the dream as a creative expression of the self, recognizing its transformative potential in the therapeutic process. According to Perls, Hefferline, and Goodman, the dream should not be analyzed rationally but fully experienced through concentration and the flow of awareness it fosters. This implies exploring and reliving the dream contents through the id, the mode of the self that encourages the emergence of repressed excitations, allowing images and emotions to manifest and transform spontaneously.

6.4 Dreamwork and the Continuum of Awareness: A Clinical Technique

The approach to working with dreams that I intend to present involves applying the technique of concentration to both the entire dream and specific aspects or details. As we have seen, in *Ego, Hunger and Aggression,* Perls suggests describing a single dream image in detail, considering it in its static form. In *Gestalt Therapy*, Perls, Hefferline, and Goodman suggest exploring the dream image through literary and pictorial representation, emphasizing the aesthetic, sensory, and pre-verbal aspects of the dream. If, instead, we examine the entire dream rather than a single image, attention can focus not on a static element but on a dynamically evolving situation. We can then grasp not only the images of the dream but also other elements such as action, the development of emotional tension, conflict, conclusion, interruption, and so on. The focus, in any case, is not on the meaning of the dream or its elements but on how, starting from any detail, a new figure is constructed. What matters is what the patient does with the dream, or with some of its aspects, in the present moment of the encounter with the therapist.

The method I am about to describe is a practical application of the id in therapeutic work, based on the continuum of awareness. First, the patient will be asked to recount the dream in the present tense, as if they were experiencing it at that moment, to make the experience more vivid and facilitate their immersion. Once the patient has recounted the dream, the therapist will give the following instructions:

> Close your eyes and mentally retrace the dream, like a film projected in your mind. Observe the various elements of the dream—images, colors, words, phrases, emotions, or anything else—and notice which one attracts your attention the most. Describe it in detail, stay focused on it, and observe how it evolves spontaneously. Sensations, emotions, images, thoughts may emerge... Simply observe what happens, allowing everything to occur spontaneously.

Focusing attention on the emerging aspects of the dream will spontaneously give rise to the process of forming the dynamic figure–ground relationship. The initial figure will evolve and change, becoming the background for a new figure. In this way, a succession of experiences will be generated: images, physical sensations, emotions, thoughts, memories. It is advisable not to expect striking results. The goal is not to anticipate something extraordinary happening but rather to try and see if something emerges and, if so, what. It might also be that not much happens. The reactions of different patients, or of the same patient at different times, can vary significantly, "from virtually none to important unblockings of excitement" (Perls *et al.*, 1994, p. 413). However, often, concentration, even on a simple physical sensation, can trigger a chain of internal events.

The therapist invites the patient to focus attention on the figure that emerges each time and to wait for it to develop further, saying, for example: "Stay with this, breathe, and see what happens." By suggesting that the patient breathe, the therapist encourages them to slightly accelerate and expand their breathing rhythm. In this way, modifying the breathing rhythm intensifies excitement and facilitates the emergence of a new figure.

The therapist's almost pressing rhythm of questions between one event and another ("What do you notice now? What is happening? What is emerging at this moment?") accelerates the sequence of experiences and prevents the patient from pausing. In this way, the therapist guides the process, "controlling the nature of the sequences so that one experience runs right into another and discrete units lose their identity" (Polster, 1987, p. 65). The result is "a sharply directed concentration, much as we see in hypnosis or meditation" (1987, p. 66).

One event spontaneously follows another, and if nothing interrupts it, the process flows smoothly, releasing waves of emotions and discharging repressed energy. The patient continues to focus on the various moments of the experience and to describe their awareness of them. The therapist minimizes their interventions, limiting them to those aimed at facilitating the ongoing process and bringing it back to its spontaneous flow when it is interrupted. As long as the process flows naturally, the therapist intervenes only to invite the patient to focus on the current figure, the one that has most recently emerged. Sometimes they may confirm, emphasize, or encourage what the patient expresses through nonverbal signals, such as smiles or nods, or with vocalizations or words like "ah," "uhm," "yes," "good." They avoid highlighting, through verbalizations or reformulations, emotions or cognitive content that seem more central or significant than others, so as not to interfere with the spontaneous evolution of the patient's experience. If, for example, the patient lingers on making a series of considerations on a theme, at the end, the therapist will simply ask them to focus on what they have just said, allowing the patient to grasp the most salient aspects on which to focus to resume the spontaneous flow of the process.

Sometimes, cognitive content can constitute a form of avoidance of the here-and-now experience, of pure sensations and emotions. However, as Polster (1987) states, thinking can also be useful in orienting us, connecting events, and can serve as a preparatory step for further developments. The flow of experiences that emerges from disinterested concentration, facilitated by relaxation and the non-integration of the self, allows the patient to perceive their experience with particular clarity, as if the mind expands and manages to grasp new connections and meanings. In this state, thanks to the integrative power of the id, the patient can achieve moments of insight, through which they gain a greater understanding of themselves and see things from a new perspective.

The natural flow of the process can be hindered by difficulties that slow it down or block it. The patient may stop at a certain point and be unable to move forward, or they may deviate, taking a direction distant from what is happening. It is not always easy, at least initially, to distinguish whether a digression represents simply a phase of the sequence—whose connection to the ongoing process is not immediately evident—or whether it constitutes an interruption of the flow of awareness.

When the process is interrupted due to a block or a digression, the therapist can intervene in various ways: they can explore how the patient experiences the block; they can acknowledge the digression and then invite the patient to focus on the physical sensations of the moment; or they can suggest that the patient bring attention back to the last element that emerged before the interruption.

Where does the continuum of awareness lead? And what is the aim of dreamwork through concentration? Michael Vincent Miller answers the first question as follows:

> When you stay with and ride such sequences, which sometimes can be like riding a bucking bronco, and sometimes like driving a sports car on an open highway, you will find that all roads lead to Rome. In other words, you can begin any place in therapy, and if you follow the process, you get to the heart of the matter. But the question remains: what is "Rome"? I would argue that Rome is neither the core of the personality nor the authentic self, nor even the important past traumas, though such issues might arise and become important on the way to Rome. What I would say is that Rome doesn't yet exist; it has to be made. The process of staying with the experience plays a central part in what one makes.
>
> (Miller, 2003, p. 254)

The goal of the continuum of awareness, therefore, according to Miller, is an ever-open task, something that never reaches a definitive completion and that, precisely for this reason, remains alive and interesting. If, as Miller states, the starting point of the process is not decisive, it is also true that starting from a dream element adds a peculiar quality to the process itself, since, as seen in the previous paragraph, it favors contact with the archaic dimension of childhood.

According to Perls, Hefferline, and Goodman, dreamwork through concentration aims to expand awareness and promote the integrated functioning of the person. The process can also lead to the recovery of specific memories, but this is only a secondary effect. The main objective is to foster the individual's creative power and encourage greater integration of their experience through the discovery and release of blocked energy.

At a certain point, the sequence of events might favor the ongoing interaction between patient and therapist, bringing out, for example, something the patient wishes to express or do toward the therapist. It is essential that the latter knows how to recognize and support this search for direct contact. As Spagnuolo Lobb (2013, p. 125) states, what the patient talks about always implies an intentionality of contact with the therapist: "The patient's narration to the therapist is for us Gestaltists (hence phenomenological-relational therapists) a creative act by means of which the patient attempts to overcome, in the contact with the therapist, unsatisfactory relational patterns learned in previous relationships." The main task of the therapist is, therefore, to welcome and support this intentionality. The core of healing lies in the encounter that takes place in the here and now between therapist and patient. It would be a mistake to continue working solely on awareness when what the patient truly needs is to make contact and feel met by the therapist.

Dreamwork, through the continuum of awareness, can conclude when the therapist senses that something new has occurred in the patient's experience: a change, even minimal, but significant for the ongoing developmental process. If conducted correctly, the described procedure tends to leave the patient with a sense of relief, a feeling of well-being, and an increased ability to perceive the situation from a broader perspective.

6.5 A Clinical Example: Retroflection, Trust, and Contact

The following clinical example illustrates the application of the dreamwork method based on concentration and the continuum of awareness, as outlined in the previous section. In this case, the therapeutic process unfolds through the patient's focused attention on specific dream elements, bodily sensations, and emotional responses emerging in the here and now. This approach, rooted in the mode of functioning of the id, facilitates the emergence of meaningful experiences and supports a movement toward integration and spontaneous contact.

The patient is 29 years old, in therapy with me for six months following a previous two-year therapeutic experience with another professional. Her contact style is predominantly retroflective: accustomed to being seen as strong and a point of reference for her family, both for her sisters and parents, she tends to exercise strict control over her emotions and perceives the environment as needing care rather than being capable of caring for her. For the past few weeks, she has been living with her partner.

In the transcript of the following session, the patient primarily expresses difficulty in fully trusting the environment. In her current situation, she experiences the possibility of letting go and making emotional requests, albeit in a conflicted manner, as closeness provokes anxiety.

The patient recounts the following dream, experienced the previous night:

Patient (P): I am with a group of work colleagues. The atmosphere is very serene. I notice the face of a colleague who is also a dear friend. Then I see a woman and a child. I realize that the woman is my office manager, and she is holding not a boy but a girl. I take the girl in my arms, and she seems visibly happy to be with me. I'm pleased that the mother notices the immediate bond between me and her daughter.

Now the scene changes. I am with my boyfriend. In front of us, an iguana appears. I am behind my boyfriend and feel scared; I sense that the iguana is there for me. At a certain point, the iguana jumps towards us; my boyfriend moves aside and lets the iguana land on me.

Therapist (T): Close your eyes, try to mentally revisit the entire dream, and see what stands out to you the most.

P: (Closes her eyes. She keeps them closed throughout the session.) I'm struck by the image of the child; he's beautiful, soft, I want to hold him.

T: Focus on this image, observe it in detail, and see what happens.

P: Now his mother also seems more beautiful... Now I see another little girl, whom I met last Sunday; it moves me... My boyfriend is also here. I tell him: "This little girl is beautiful." And he says: "Yes, she is beautiful. Only you are more beautiful than her." "That's not true, she's more beautiful than me"... Now the images become blurry, I see darkness, there's a shadow; it's my mother, I feel like crying even more... Now my mother is gone, my father has appeared... Now he's gone too... I see my boyfriend moving aside and the iguana jumping on me, but I'm not afraid; I manage to push it away, it doesn't terrify me, it's as if it were a cockroach.

T: Try to focus on the image of your boyfriend moving aside and the iguana jumping on you.

[The previous passage presents several significant contents. I invite the patient, following an exclusively chronological criterion, to focus on the scene that emerged last.]

P: I scold him. It comes to mind that when there are dogs and I ask him to stay close to me, he stays close only with those I'm not afraid of. But when there are dogs that scare me, he's not there: he says that before he even has time to come closer, I've already run away. So he stays close only when I don't need it. I feel bad saying this because I know he tries, but I wish he could read my mind... When I'm here, I always feel my bladder is full.

T: Focus on this sensation.

P: Strange, if I focus on the sensation in my bladder, instead of increasing, it decreases! (Pause.)

T: What's happening now?

P: Now I feel a strange tingling in my hand; it's heavy, as if I had a glove on. I'm getting anxious, as if I had an IV in my arm. (Her breathing becomes heavy, labored.)... Thoughts related to sex come to mind... (She opens and closes her right hand.) If I don't open and close it, I can't feel it anymore... I have the feeling that the movement of my hand is somehow connected to sex... If I grip the armrest of the chair, I feel better... I feel my right arm stiff...

I feel my bladder again... My left arm is fine, but my right arm feels swollen, numb. It's as if I have no sensation in my fingertips... I had a flash, a terrible thing I saw yesterday: the electric chair ride at the amusement park... I feel like I'm on an electric chair... My right hand is big, monstrous; the left one is normal... The palm of my right hand is burning.

T: Focus on this sensation.

P: Now my hand feels the opposite of before: small and weak. ... An image of a hanged person comes to mind.

T: Focus on this image.

P: I see him hanging. ... Now I don't see anything. ... Now it's as if I'm on a boat and touching the water. ... I felt something like a cockroach on my right arm. ... (She curls up in the chair.) I like being like this; it reminds me of a session in my previous therapy. I had positioned myself this way, and the therapist was observing me, trying to understand what it meant. I feel like slouching. ... I feel a heaviness in my chest. A strange thought came to mind; the idea of telling you makes me anxious.

T: Feel free to share it or not.

P: I feel you're distant, sitting over there, and I wish you were closer.

T.: Imagine I'm sitting here, next to you. What happens?

P: I feel a tightening around my neck.

T: Focus on this sensation.

P: It's not you who's squeezing me. ... It hurts. I feel this sensation only on one side of my neck, only on the left, as if my throat were split in two. ... Now I have the feeling that the chair next to me is empty, as if you had gotten up and left. ... Now my head hurts.

T: We have a few more minutes before we conclude.

P: I feel like when I have to get up in the morning and say, "Just two more minutes!" ... During this session, I mostly felt negative sensations, yet I feel so good now! (She opens her eyes.) What happened? Strange! I feel like when I wake up in the morning. But I feel good.

When we meet again a week later, she tells me she left the previous session feeling particularly well, calm, and satisfied. Throughout the day, she was accompanied by a sense of spontaneity and openness, which eventually led her to discuss with her partner a topic she had previously avoided: her desire to get married rather than just live together.

The interpretations presented in the following comment make no claim to truth or validity, but are solely intended to illustrate the developments that may emerge from applying concentration to the dream material, as well as the meanings these developments could take on. Within the phenomenological framework of Gestalt therapy, valid therapeutic meanings are those that the patient reaches on their own, those that emerge directly from their experience.

In the initial part of this work, the patient revisits and develops some content of the dream, related to the current phase of her life cycle, characterized by the conflict between attachment to the past and the evolutionary impulses of the present. On one hand, the patient confronts the prospect of motherhood, which attracts her: "I'm struck by the image of the child; he's beautiful, soft, I want to hold him." On the other hand, she feels the pain of separation from her childhood ("Now I see another little girl, it moves me") and from her parents ("There's a shadow, it's my mother, I feel like crying even more... Now my mother is no longer here, my father has appeared... Now he's gone too"). She feels valued as a woman by her partner ("Only you are more beautiful than her"), but she fears fully trusting him. It is precisely on the difficulty of trusting, typical of the retroflective contact mode, that the remainder of the work focuses. Through a series of different physical sensations, the anxiety related to the desire to trust and let go emerges. The sexual fantasies that appear at a certain point in the work can be read as an expression of this desire, but they provoke strong resistance in her. This causes her to stiffen, to not let go ("If I grab the armrest of the chair, I feel better") and first evokes the sensation of being in an electric chair, then the image of a hanged person. The subsequent fantasy of being in a boat and touching the water indicates an initial moment of relaxation. But anxiety immediately reemerges, and the patient stiffens again ("I felt something like a cockroach on my right arm").

Finally, she manages to let go and snuggles into the chair. At this point, the focus of the work shifts to our relationship: she expresses a desire for physical closeness. This request marks a turning point in the work, the dissolution of a retroflection. Sensing that it would be premature to actually get closer to her, I limit myself to suggesting she imagine it. Just imagining me sitting next to her still evokes anxiety ("I feel a tightness around my neck"). However, when I inform her that our time is about to end, something significant has already occurred in her experience: a contact has been made. The patient concludes by saying that she feels good. She will carry with her, outside of the session, a sense of greater freedom and energy. In line with the contact finally established during the session—where she allowed herself to express the need for closeness and be heard—she will, later that same day, share with her partner a desire that had until then remained unspoken. In doing so, she enacts in real life the previously missed contact that the dream had symbolically portrayed.[3]

6.6 Conclusions

The dream approach based on the continuum of awareness, presented here, is a phenomenological method, as it considers the dream as remembered and narrated by the patient, with its images, language, and magic. It does not aim to interpret the hidden meaning but to facilitate immediate contact with the dream experience, enriching the patient's lived experience. It is a nondirective method: the therapist facilitates the spontaneous development of the process without directing its course. It is centered on the id rather than the ego, promoting access to the subject's deep experience and the emergence of unfinished situations relegated to the background of awareness.

This approach differs from the dreamwork methods of Fritz Perls and Isadore From in several ways, while sharing with them the goal of promoting integration and self-awareness.

Perls considered each element of the dream as a projection of split parts of the dreamer. His method involved the patient identifying with various elements of the dream to reintegrate these parts. The main objective of this process is to allow the patient to reclaim alienated aspects of their personality.

From proposed a relational perspective, interpreting the dream as a form of retroflection. In this view, the dream reflects what the patient withholds or avoids expressing in the therapeutic relationship. Remembering and recounting the dream in therapy indicates an attempt to resolve this retroflection. This method emphasizes the relational dimension and the disturbances of the contact-boundary between patient and therapist.

The method based on the continuum of awareness invites the patient to focus on the images, sensations, and emotions evoked by the dream in the here and now, without seeking to attribute them a hidden meaning. This approach aims to facilitate the emergence of unfinished situations, activating the integrative potential of the self.

The alternation and integration of these methods, based on the context and the patient's needs, can enrich the therapeutic process, offering diverse pathways for the exploration and processing of dream material. For example, the active identification with parts of the dream, proposed by Perls, can be useful for exploring denied or unknown aspects of the self, especially in patients who require a more dynamic and concrete experience. From's attention to the relational dimension can help explore how the dream content reflects current dynamics in the therapeutic relationship. Finally, the method based on the continuum of awareness can facilitate the spontaneous emergence of repressed content, offering a deeper experience. The choice of the most appropriate method or combination of methods should be guided by the therapist's sensitivity and the specific needs of the patient in the present moment.

Notes

1 Modified and expanded version of a paper previously published in *Quaderni di Gestalt*, 2011, XXIV, 1: 35–44. https://doi.org/10.3280/GEST2011-001004.
2 Perls had already addressed the projective nature of certain dream elements in *Ego, Hunger and Aggression* (1947/1969, p. 240), where he distinguishes between two types of dreams: pleasant ones, which complete unfinished situations, and unpleasant ones, which are attributable to projections of unacceptable parts of the person.
3 The emerging processes described here should be considered not only as the result of the patient's intrapsychic processing but also as an expression of the organism/environment

field. They are the outcome of the encounter between patient and therapist in the here and now of the session. Antonio Sichera (2003, p. 98) writes: "The portrayal of the dream, in the presence of and together with the therapist, puts the dream itself into the circuit of the relationship, in the development of the present experience between an I and a Thou." For the Gestalt therapist, the relational dimension remains the primary hermeneutic criterion, even when employing an individual-centered technique, such as the one proposed here.

References

Kitzler, R. (2003). Creativity as Gestalt therapy. In M. Spagnuolo Lobb & N. Amendt-Lyon (Eds.), *Creative license: The art of Gestalt therapy* (pp. 101–111). Wien/New York, NY: Springer.

Macaluso, M. A. (2011). L'uso della concentrazione nel lavoro sui sogni in psicoterapia della Gestalt. *Quaderni di Gestalt*, 24(1), 35–44. https://doi.org/10.3280/GEST2011-001004

Miller, M. V. (2003). The aesthetics of commitment: What Gestalt therapists can learn from Cézanne and Miles Davis. In M. Spagnuolo Lobb & N. Amendt-Lyon (Eds.), *Creative license: The art of Gestalt therapy* (pp. 153–161). Wien/New York, NY: Springer.

Perls, F. (1969). *Gestalt therapy verbatim*. Moab, UT: Real People Press.

Perls, F. (1969). *Ego, hunger and aggression: The beginning of Gestalt therapy*. New York: Vintage Books (Random House). (Original work published 1947).

Perls, F., Hefferline, R., & Goodman, P. (1951/1994). *Gestalt therapy: Excitement and growth in the human personality*. Highland, NY: The Gestalt Journal Press.

Polster, E. (1987). *Every person's life is worth a novel*. Highland, NY: The Gestalt Journal Press.

Rosenfeld, E. (1978). An oral history of Gestalt therapy: Part II: A conversation with Isadore From. *The Gestalt Journal*, 1(2), 7–27.

Sichera, A. (2003). Therapy as an aesthetic issue: Creativity, dreams, and art in Gestalt therapy. In M. Spagnuolo Lobb & N. Amendt-Lyon (Eds.), *Creative license: The art of Gestalt therapy* (pp. 93–99). Wien/New York, NY: Springer.

Spagnuolo Lobb, M. (2013). *The now-for-next in psychotherapy: Gestalt therapy recounted in post-modern society*. Milano: FrancoAngeli. (Original work published 2011 as *Il now-for-next in psicoterapia*, Milano: FrancoAngeli).

Chapter 7

Personality, Neurotic Mechanisms, and Gestalt Diagnosis

7.1 Introduction

The concept of *personality* occupies a central place in the Gestalt theoretical model, as highlighted by the title of the fundamental text on Gestalt therapy: *Gestalt Therapy: Excitement and Growth in the Human Personality* (Perls *et al.*, 1951/1994), which emphasizes the importance of personality in the growth process. Personality is the system of attitudes that develops through experiences and social interactions. The authors of *Gestalt Therapy* conceive it not as a static entity, but as a dynamic process that constantly evolves through interactions with the environment and the assimilation of past experiences. It represents the aspect of the self where the past and present meet, influencing current contact and providing coherence to identity. Personality allows the self to respond to the present situation by drawing on resources from the past.

The neurotic and dysfunctional aspect of personality is represented by *character*, which hinders self-regulation and spontaneity, limiting creative adjustment. The types of neurotic characters described by Perls, Hefferline, and Goodman correspond to the main *neurotic mechanisms*, also called *interruptions of contact* or *resistances*. These mechanisms are understood by the authors of *Gestalt Therapy* as interruptions in the process of creative adjustment, caused by removals in the ground of experience.

Both Wheeler (1991) and Spagnuolo Lobb (2013) have proposed, in different ways, a revision of these mechanisms, which involves a re-reading of the very concept of contact and an enhancement of the individual ground, made up of acquired past experiences. Both authors emphasize the role of the individual ground as an integral part of the self-process.

After describing personality as a system of attitudes and modes of the contact process, I will discuss the mechanisms underlying the different neurotic characters and the revisions proposed by Wheeler and Spagnuolo Lobb. In the final section of this chapter, I will present some considerations on Gestalt diagnosis, arguing that it should consider not only the current contact process but also the patient's ground of experience, that is, their personality.

DOI: 10.4324/9781003726753-8

7.2 Personality as a System of Attitudes

Perls, Hefferline, and Goodman (1994, p. 160) define personality as "the system of attitudes assumed in interpersonal relations." It develops through creative interaction with others, in which the individual imitates and identifies with them, creating a self-image influenced by received models. Personality represents the way we recognize ourselves and present ourselves to others; it is "the assumption of what one is" (1994, p. 160) and provides a basis for interpreting our behavior.

Perls, Hefferline, and Goodman describe personality as a "structure of speech habits" and a "verbal replica of the self" (1994, pp. 100, 160), thus emphasizing the significant role of language in expressing who we are (1994, p. 130). Essentially, in their view, personality is expressed through the linguistic habits we use to describe ourselves and relate to others, making language a fundamental tool for representing our identity. This perspective anticipates, at least in part, the notion of *narrative identity*, according to which the individual constructs the self through the stories they tell about themselves, organizing lived experience into a coherent and shareable form.[1]

The neurotic aspect of personality is *character*, conceived as a fixed form of the personality—that is, a rigid and persistent structure that manifests in the present but originates from unassimilated past experiences. Character is expressed through repetitive behaviors that are often inadequate in meeting the needs of the current situation. It is this rigidity that makes character a neurotic element of personality, as it hinders adaptation and self-regulation in the present.

Perls, Hefferline, and Goodman emphasize that aspects of character persist only as long as they serve a useful function in the present. A characteristic, even a neurotic one, remains active only if the organism perceives that it somehow plays a role in the present. However, when these structures become useless, the organism tends to discard them through self-regulation: what is no longer needed is forgotten or "dissolved." In other words, what persists does so not out of inertia but because it maintains an active role in the present.

In a well-known passage from *Gestalt Therapy*, Perls, Hefferline, and Goodman state that the ideal condition is to have little personality, to be flexible and adaptable, like water, which, according to a Taoist maxim, takes the shape of the container that holds it. Here, the term *personality* should be understood in the narrow sense of *character*. When the self is burdened by many unresolved situations, chronic inhibitions, introjects, mistaken self-conceptions, recurring rigid attitudes, destructive loyalties—all aspects that constitute character—the person responds to the present situation not in a flexible and creative way but based on incorporated alien material. In healthy functioning, on the other hand, the self remains open to learning and continuous change, without fixating on a stable or rigid identity.

Character is only a part of personality, which also includes functional fixed forms that support relational competence and *personal style*—each individual's unique way of being, feeling, and thinking. Laura Perls (1976/1997, p. 222) defines *style* as "a unified integrated way of expression and communication." In this sense, personal style reflects the level of development a person has achieved and supports the current process. Unlike character, which is a rigid structure that hinders awareness and growth, it is flexible and subject to change.

7.3 Personality as a Mode of the Contact Process

Perls, Hefferline, and Goodman propose a conception of personality as a dynamic and complex process, in which both past experiences (acquired attitudes) and responses to the demands of the present moment intertwine. For them, personality is not a static structure but a constantly evolving system, capable of drawing from the past as a resource to creatively adapt to the current context.

When the self operates in an integrated and spontaneous manner, Perls, Hefferline, and Goodman state, personality corresponds to the final phase of the process—the post-contact phase—where the newly encountered experience is assimilated and becomes part of the organism. In this sense, personality is what we become through the assimilation of lived experience. However, according to the authors of *Gestalt Therapy*—as discussed in Chapter 2 of this book—it is not appropriate to use the terms *id*, *ego*, and *personality* to designate the phases of development of the spontaneous self. According to Perls, Hefferline, and Goodman, these terms refer instead to specific modes of self-functioning, defined as "partial structures of the self." In particular, the authors refer to personality as the mode of contact through which the self engages with the environment based on assimilated experiences.

The following example, concerning a person learning to overcome the difficulty of speaking in public, illustrates personality as a way of contacting the environment based on assimilated experiences. Imagine that this person initially experiences strong anxiety and shyness in social situations, especially when speaking in front of an audience. They then decide to gradually expose themselves to situations that involve public speaking, facing their fear and developing new communication skills. With each experience, the self comes into contact with the *novelty* of speaking in public and, in the post-contact phase, assimilates what has been learned, progressively integrating these experiences into their way of being.

This transformation is not just about acquiring skills, but also about creatively adjusting to new experiences and situations and integrating them into one's identity.

Over time, public speaking becomes a natural part of their functioning: anxiety decreases, and the acquired skills become integrated into their personality. Now, the person can respond spontaneously and confidently in situations that require them to express themselves in front of an audience. Their *personality* has changed and expanded through the assimilation of these lived experiences, transforming a rigid aspect of character (shyness and anxiety) into a resource for the present.

As we saw in Chapter 2, Perls, Hefferline, and Goodman define personality as *autonomous*, *responsible*, and *transparent*. Here, I return to the concept of *autonomy*, which particularly characterizes personality, implying the self-sufficiency of the self in making decisions and responding to the demands of the present. In this context, the term *autonomy*, of Greek origin, should be understood in its etymological sense. It derives from the words αὐτός (self) and νόμος (law). In the autonomous functioning of personality, the accumulated past experiences—i.e., what the person is (αὐτός)—become the criterion (νόμος) by which present experience is organized. In other words, the self structures itself autonomously based on internal criteria, derived from lived experiences, rather than external ones. When the self operates in this way, experience does not necessarily represent something new, but rather something consistent with what the individual has already assimilated: it is the reflection of their personality, their personal style. Autonomy also enables transparent and responsible behavior, as the individual, self-aware, is able to fully take responsibility for their choices.

7.4 Personality and the Therapeutic Situation

After discussing the role of spontaneity, intentionality, and relaxation in the therapeutic situation in previous chapters, I will now focus on the role of personality. Erving Polster emphasizes that every Gestalt therapist interprets Gestalt therapy according to their own style:

> Regarding the application of theory, it is essential to consider not only its accuracy and connotations but also the priorities that the therapist assigns to certain aspects of the theory over others. In this context, the concept of therapeutic style (or repertoire) emerges. Within Gestalt therapy, some therapists focus on improving the quality of contact, others on clarifying and expanding awareness, while others primarily use experiments. For example, there is a group of professionals who work exclusively with the empty chair technique. Although these approaches may seem limited, they can be understood as expressions of a distinctive style. Through stylistic characterization, every individual—whether a therapist or an artist—is able to generate a series of meaningful events within their own stylistic framework. Another individual might never be able to operate in that particular style, no matter how correct they may consider it to be.
>
> (Polster, 1986, p. 65).[2]

There are as many Gestalt therapies as there are Gestalt therapists. This is true not only because each therapist applies the Gestalt model differently according to their personal style but also, and above all, because the therapist uses themselves as an instrument of intervention. The therapist's authenticity is fundamental; they help the patient by being themselves, responding to the other with their own professional skills and life experiences. As Laura Perls (1976/1997, p. 223) writes: "A Gestalt therapist does not use techniques; he applies *himself in* and *to* a situation with whatever professional skills and life experience he has accumulated and integrated." This approach implies that every therapeutic relationship is unique, the result of mutual discovery between therapist and patient, who together create a shared path of growth.

7.5 Mechanisms and Neurotic Characters

Let us now return to examining the neurotic aspects of personality, which, as previously emphasized, constitute character. Perls, Hefferline, and Goodman write (1994, p. 209): "Neurotic behavior is [...] a learned habit." Therefore, the neurotic functioning observable in the present moment in a person represents a characteristic and habitual mode of their behavior—an aspect of their character. The description of the main *neurotic mechanisms* provided by Perls, Hefferline, and Goodman thus constitutes a typology of characters.

In this section, I will first examine the main neurotic mechanisms, understood as interruptions of the creative adjustment process that lead to the loss of ego functions, according to the original Gestalt model. Subsequently, I will consider some revisions of these mechanisms, proposed by Wheeler (1991) and Spagnuolo Lobb (2013), which offer important implications for diagnosis in Gestalt therapy.

7.5.1 Neurotic Mechanisms as Interruptions of the Contact Process

The authors of *Gestalt Therapy* state: "Neurotic behaviors are creative adjustments of a field in which there are repressions" (Perls *et al.*, 1994, p. 227). The background of neurotic experience contains repressions—that is, chronic and unaware inhibitions that interfere with the current process of creative adjustment, interrupting the excitement that accompanies this process. These interruptions are defined by Perls, Hefferline, and Goodman as *neurotic mechanisms*, using terminology clearly borrowed from psychoanalysis. The various neurotic mechanisms can be considered "as the stages of creative adjustment at which the excitement is interrupted" (1994, p. 228). Depending on the stage at which the interruption occurs in the process, a specific type of neurotic mechanism will emerge. Below, we will briefly examine the main mechanisms that, according to Perls, Hefferline, and Goodman, are the most significant, though not the only ones.[3]

Confluence: The figure/ground formation process does not even begin. The person perceives no excitement, no stimulus; they are almost paralyzed and wait for the other to act.

Introjection: The interruption occurs when excitement arises due to the emergence of a need that, consequently, is not recognized. Instead of identifying with their own need, the person identifies with the environment.

Projection: Excitement is suppressed when the organism faces the environment and the emotion intensifies. The emotion is not recognized and is instead attributed to the other.

Retroflection: The process is interrupted at the moment of conflict, during the phase in which a part of the environment is destroyed.[4] Aggression, originally directed toward the environment, is redirected toward the self.
Egotism: Excitement is blocked at the final moment, at the peak of contact, when the person should let go, taking something from the environment and giving something back to it.

Each of these mechanisms corresponds to a specific character, that is, a particular habitual attitude toward both the organism itself and the environment. However, Perls, Hefferline, and Goodman emphasize that the typology they propose is a tool aimed not at classifying the individual's overall character but rather at describing a single neurotic experience. Although one type of interruption may be predominant, manifesting more frequently and evidently, according to Perls, Hefferline, and Goodman, a person's character cannot be reduced to a single type of interruption, as the individual does not possess just one type but rather all of them, using them at different moments. Even within the same experience, different types of interruptions can emerge, either sequentially or in combination with one another.

According to the authors of *Gestalt Therapy*, the phenomenological approach they propose focuses on present experience in its concreteness and does not aim to assign a diagnosis that defines the patient's character. The diagnosis proposed by Perls, Hefferline, and Goodman serves the understanding of the experience in progress. It helps us to precisely describe how and when the process is interrupted in the current situation. And since a detailed description of present experience through focused awareness activates the self and promotes its integration, this type of diagnosis is closely linked to therapy and, in a certain sense, coincides with it.

7.5.2 Neurotic Mechanisms as a Loss of Ego Functions

The interrupted excitement, a phenomenon often accompanied by an alteration in breathing, generates anxiety and prevents the normal progression of the process. The experience, thus suffocated, cannot reach the fullness of final contact. The expression *interruption of contact* indicates that the contact process, while continuing, loses energy and clarity, thus proceeding with reduced awareness.[5]

In the neurotic experience, the interruption of excitement, caused by the interference of repression, leads to the loss of ego functions. Perls, Hefferline, and Goodman define neurosis as a loss of ego functions, meaning a decrease in the ability to orient oneself and to act creatively and effectively. This loss specifically affects the ego's orienting and manipulating functions, which are crucial for maintaining a flexible and coherent adaptation to the environment. When these functions are compromised, the organism's responses become either rigid or confused, leading to neurotic patterns of contact. The functioning of the ego essentially consists in establishing the boundaries of experience, drawing lines of demarcation between the desires, interests, and powers of the self. On one side of the demarcation line lies what is interesting and with which one identifies; on the other side is what lacks interest and is alienated. In a healthy experience, these boundaries are well-defined yet flexible, varying according to interest, need, or will at the moment.

In the neurotic experience, Perls, Hefferline, and Goodman (1994, p. 228) identify two opposing conditions of boundaries, which correspond to two different ways of losing ego functions:

> The neurotic loses his boundaries, his sense of where he is and what and how he is doing, and he can no longer cope, or he feels his boundaries as inflexibly fixed, he does not get on, and he can no longer cope.

On one side, there is the absence of demarcation lines in contact—confluence—which means the avoidance of differentiation and autonomy. On the other side, there is the rigidity of these demarcation lines, leading to egotistic fixation and the avoidance of intimacy. Every neurotic experience tends toward one of these two extremes: confluence, typical of the hysterical experience, or fixation, characteristic of compulsive experience.[6]

The following example illustrates a situation of loss of ego functions, with the manifestation of several interruptions in sequence. Imagine a person who feels anxious while parking a car. As soon as they begin the maneuver, they feel agitated, contract their abdominal muscles, clench their teeth, and hold their breath (retroflection). Their clarity decreases, and they become impulsive and clumsy, misjudging the entry into the parking space. This increases their heart rate and agitation. If another car stops behind them waiting, their agitation grows even more. They think that the other driver is judging them as clumsy (projection) and internalize this judgment (introjection), feeling ashamed. The urgency to finish increases, leading to a crescendo of confusion and desensitization, progressively losing contact with present reality.

The loss of ego functions in the neurotic experience is not total: "The neurotic self has lost part of its ego-functions" (Perls *et al.*, 1994, p. 213). The neurotic experience remains, nonetheless, a creative adjustment. As such, it is still a form of contact. It is an imperfect mode of contact in which the self does its best to find creative solutions, given the circumstances and the resources at its disposal. Perls *et al.* (1994, p. 153) write: "The areas of contact may be restricted, as in the neuroses, but wherever there is a boundary and contact occurs, it is, in so far, creative self." In this sense, the interruption of contact, typical of the neurotic condition, can be considered a particular form of contact, characterized by a disturbance of awareness and a reduced ability to be present in the "here and now." Even though this contact is incomplete and less satisfying compared to a full contact experience, it still provides a positive, albeit partial, satisfaction.

The interruptions in the contact process have often been described as *contact disturbances* or *forms of resistance*, highlighting only their dysfunctional aspect. It is true that they play an important role in the formation of neurotic symptoms; however, in themselves, they do not constitute pathological mechanisms. Excitement can be interrupted in response to an unavoidable situation of danger or frustration, which Perls, Hefferline, and Goodman define as an *acute emergency*, without this necessarily implying a loss of ego functions. In such cases, the self continues to function in a healthy way, seeking creative solutions as best as possible, given the obstacles it encounters. In themselves, interruptions in the contact process are adaptive functions; they represent the imperfect contact that is possible in certain situations. They become pathological when, being associated with repression, they become chronic and lead to a loss of ego functions.

The loss of ego functions implies a reduction in the vitality of the self. This is the quality that distinguishes a healthy experience from a neurotic one. The vitality of *good contact* manifests through "specific observable properties of brightness, clarity, unity, fascination, grace, vigor, release, etc., depending on whether we are considering primarily a perceptual, feelingful, or motor context" (Perls *et al.*, 1994, p. 8). These qualities, of an "aesthetic" nature, serve as useful indicators for the diagnostic evaluation of experience. They are not based on comparison with a standard of normality or health but are intrinsic to the experience itself. These criteria can be used not only by the therapist, through observation, but also by the patient, to develop a greater awareness of their sensations and experiences.

Gestalt therapy does not aim to modify behavior based on an ideal model of health, nor to correct dysfunctions in the current process, but rather to foster its spontaneous development through the organism's self-regulation. It is, therefore, "a method not of correction but of growth" (Perls *et al.*, 1994, p. 14). In the Gestalt perspective, the protagonist of the therapeutic process is not the therapist, but the patient. The latter is the true expert of their own experience: they can evaluate it based on what they feel and, with some support, develop their potential, their vital and creative self. Perls, Hefferline, and Goodman thus propose an approach to the evaluation and treatment of human suffering that moves away from the traditional medical model, emphasizing the subjectivity of experience and the transformative power of contact.

In conclusion, neurosis, according to Perls, Hefferline, and Goodman, does not represent a total loss of contact, but rather an imperfect and partial mode in which the self still attempts to adapt creatively to circumstances. The interruption of contact, though accompanied by a partial loss of ego functions, nonetheless constitutes a form of contact—albeit less vital, clear, and integrated. The aesthetic quality of experience, understood as brightness, unity, and spontaneity, emerges as an intrinsic diagnostic criterion, useful for assessing the degree of presence of the self. In this sense, Gestalt therapy does not aim to correct dysfunction, but to reactivate the process of self-regulation through an increase in awareness and vitality in the here and now.

7.5.3 New Interpretations of Neurotic Mechanisms and the Ground

The model of neurotic mechanisms developed by Perls, Hefferline, and Goodman has been widely discussed in Gestalt literature. In the first chapter of this book,

I have already referred to the reinterpretations of the concept of contact proposed by Gordon Wheeler (1991) and Margherita Spagnuolo Lobb (2013). Building upon these, both authors have suggested revisions to the traditional understanding of neurotic mechanisms, albeit through different approaches. Wheeler (1991, p. 113) observes that Gestalt neurotic mechanisms, which he defines as *resistances*, derive from psychoanalytic defense mechanisms: "The 'resistances' [...] were a direct incorporation, or introjection, on Perls's part, from psychodynamic theory."

The psychoanalytic defense mechanisms, notes Wheeler, are based on a tragic conception of human nature, seen as intrinsically divided. For Freud, man is inevitably in conflict with himself and with society. The Gestalt concept of a neurotic mechanism—understood by Perls, Hefferline, and Goodman primarily as a form of resistance to contact—diverges from Freud's pessimism by eliminating the tragic element of inner division in human nature. In Gestalt therapy, neurosis is not viewed as the result of a structural and irreconcilable conflict between parts of the psyche, but rather as an interruption in the flow of awareness, that is, in the contact process. The self is not intrinsically split, but may lose its integrative function due to repressions present in the background. In this light, resistance is not a fatal flaw, but a creative—if partial—adaptation to challenging circumstances.

However, according to Wheeler, even this divergence from Freud remains limited. He argues that the very distinction between *contact* and *resistance to contact* is inconsistent with the holistic and integrative premises of Gestalt therapy. From his perspective, what have traditionally been seen as resistances are not obstacles to contact, but rather variations or modalities through which contact itself is organized. Therefore, Wheeler proposes a revision of the classical conception of Gestalt resistances. He argues that what Perls, Hefferline, and Goodman describe as resistances to contact—or contact disturbances—are, in fact, processes and functions that constitute contact itself. According to Wheeler, their model tends to emphasize *good contact* as an ideal form, at the expense of recognizing the adaptive value of so-called resistances. In this regard, Wheeler (1991, p. 113) writes:

> There is no such thing as "contact" in some ideal, platonic form, pure and theoretical, which then in the "real" case becomes unfortunately sullied with "resistance"—confluence, projection, introjection, deflection, and all the rest. Rather, the exercise of all these modes, all these variables at the boundary, which we will call "contact functions," is contact.

In Wheeler's revised model, every contact is characterized by the use and combination of specific contact functions, which can be employed either to inhibit the ongoing process or to facilitate it. The diagnostic evaluation of the combination of functions that constitute a specific contact depends on the subject's goals and the particular circumstances of the moment.

Spagnuolo Lobb (2013) also goes beyond the traditional conception of *contact interruptions*, highlighting their functional and adaptive aspects and reinterpreting them within a framework of complexity and development. In her elaboration, the neurotic mechanisms described by Perls, Hefferline, and Goodman become domains of experience—areas of differentiated and autonomous relational competencies that develop over time through contact experiences. As relational competencies, these *domains* belong to the acquired past, to the background. By interacting with each other in different ways depending on the moment, they manifest in the present and shape the emerging figure in function of the contact with the environment. In the clinical setting, what we observe is how the patient's current relational competence, shaped by their past experiences, is actualized in the figure of the present encounter.

Both Wheeler and Spagnuolo Lobb emphasize the role of the ground in the formation of the figure. Reviewing the themes discussed in *Gestalt Reconsidered* (1991), in a later paper, Wheeler (2016) states that the ground is not a mere passive context, but a dynamic and structured system that includes an individual's past experiences, values, commitments, and relational habits. This ground interacts with the present, influencing the formation of the emerging figure in contact.

Spagnuolo Lobb (2016) introduces the concept of *experience of the ground*, referring to the active role of evolutionary and psychopathological aspects in the creation of the present figure. According to the author, the experience of the ground is a fundamental condition for the formation of the figure and is in turn influenced by it. Forms from the past, upon encountering the present process, engage in a dynamic dialogue with it. In this sense, both the figure and the ground are experiences co-created by the organism and the environment. Spagnuolo Lobb (2016) states that the ground is part of the unitary Gestalt of the self.

For Spagnuolo Lobb (2013, p. 101), the ground also serves as a diagnostic tool. She writes:

> I believe that a relational, procedural, and phenomenological approach such as that of Gestalt therapy must consider the "given" situation and hence the background of the patient's developmental experience (diachronic level) and the figure of the present malaise and of the intentionality of contact which s/he seeks to bring to completion (synchronic level).

According to Spagnuolo Lobb, therefore, the Gestalt therapist must consider not only the figure of contact co-created in the present moment between patient and therapist, but also the ground constituted by the patient's past experiences and the configuration (Gestalt) of the relational domains developed over time, which represent their current relational competence. Consistent with these premises, the author has identified and described, for diagnostic purposes, four types of ground: *neurotic*, *borderline*, *psychotic*, and *post-traumatic*.

The contemporary reinterpretation of neurotic mechanisms proposed by Wheeler and Spagnuolo Lobb enriches the Gestalt model by reframing the so-called contact interruptions or resistances as meaningful forms of contact. Rather than being viewed exclusively as dysfunctions, these processes are understood as adaptive functions, rooted in the individual's relational ground. This perspective highlights the importance of considering not only the present contact experience, but also the history of acquired relational competencies that shape it. In this light, diagnosis becomes a dynamic and situated understanding of how the figure of the present encounter is co-created by the organism and the environment, supported—and at times limited—by the ground.

7.6 Final Considerations on Gestalt Diagnosis

To conclude, a reflection on the clinical implications of the discussion developed so far regarding the issue of diagnosis is provided below. As we have seen, according to the model of Perls, Hefferline, and Goodman, Gestalt diagnosis is intrinsic. This means that evaluation does not involve comparing the experience with a standard or a reference model, but is based on internal criteria within the process itself, observing what happens in the present moment.

In the relational perspective that characterizes contemporary Gestalt therapy, diagnosis becomes a more complex issue, as it no longer only concerns the individual characteristics of the patient, but also includes an interpretation of the relational dynamics that emerge in the therapeutic encounter. In a relational perspective, I propose distinguishing between two types of intrinsic diagnosis: *relational aesthetic diagnosis* and *relational theoretical diagnosis*. Both are essential for understanding and working within the therapeutic situation, but they refer to two modes of perception and understanding of the encounter that are conceptually distinct, though not easily separable.

Relational aesthetic diagnosis is based on immediate and pre-reflective knowledge that the therapist acquires through their sensory experience and bodily awareness in the process of contact with the patient. Thanks to this experience, the therapist is able to perceive the emotional and relational dynamics that emerge in the field during the encounter. Aesthetic diagnosis represents a form of knowledge that does not pass through the filter of theoretical reflection but is based on direct and intuitive perception of the present moment.

Relational theoretical diagnosis, on the other hand, explores the interactive and reciprocal dynamics between patient and therapist, based on reflection mediated by theory. It includes the use of theoretical models to analyze how contact develops between participants. In other words, while aesthetic diagnosis focuses on sensory and immediate perception, theoretical diagnosis integrates this intuitive level with theoretical and methodological reflection.

In recent years, several authors have emphasized the importance of the sensory component in diagnosing what happens in the therapeutic encounter. Aesthetic diagnosis allows the therapist to guide their intervention moment by moment, supporting the emerging intentionality of contact immediately and spontaneously. However, it is essential to recognize that this form of knowledge, while powerful and immediate, can be influenced by the therapist's projections, personal biases, and past experiences. Moreover, an exclusively aesthetic diagnostic approach is insufficient. It must be integrated with a theoretical understanding that allows for framing relational dynamics within a broader model. Perls, Hefferline, and Goodman are very clear about the necessity of a theoretical model, stating:

> The therapist needs his conception in order to keep his bearings, to know in what direction to look. It is the acquired habit that is the background for this art as in any other art. But the problem is the same as in any art: how to use this abstraction (and therefore fixation) so as not to lose the present actuality and especially the ongoingness of the actuality?
>
> (Perls *et al.*, 1994, pp. 228)

At this point, crucial questions arise: how can we diagnose Gestalt contact process dysfunctions—i.e., the interruption or alteration of the natural flow of contact between patient and therapist—while considering their reciprocal nature? What models or reference criteria can we rely on? The classic *interruptions of contact* seem inadequate for this purpose, as they imply an individualistic perspective. If a patient does not express their anger to the therapist, to formulate a diagnosis of what is happening at the contact-boundary, we must consider not only how and when the patient interrupts the process, but also if and how the therapist is supporting the patient's free expression. Simply stating that the patient is retroflecting would be a partial and unilateral reading, as it focuses solely on the individual's experience, isolating it from the environment. From a relational perspective, diagnosing a dysfunctional moment in the process should instead consider how the patient and therapist fail to meet and realize their shared intentionality of contact.

In this context, *relational theoretical diagnosis* emerges as an essential tool for understanding dysfunctions in the contact process. To diagnose them accurately, it is crucial to identify criteria that reflect the reciprocal interaction between patient and therapist. Some of these criteria might include, for example:

- The *level of anxiety or spontaneity at the contact-boundary*: are the patient and therapist tense or relaxed in their interaction? Observing the level of mutual anxiety or spontaneity provides indications about the state of the therapeutic relationship and any difficulties or openings in the contact process. For example, if the therapist notices that both they and the patient are very formal and restrained (tension), they might hypothesize that there is an avoidance of some emotion or significant theme at that moment. In this case, the therapist might try to lighten the situation by adopting a more informal tone or making a light observation, or by inviting the patient to explore what makes contact difficult at that moment. Conversely, moments of spontaneous smiling, bodily relaxation, and fluid dialogue indicate that the interaction is allowing for good contact.
- *Figure/ground dynamics*: how does the experience develop in the therapeutic process? The way in which the patient and therapist co-create new figures can be an indicator of the vitality of the relational field. Observing how figure and ground form and transform in dialogue, gestures, and emotions is a good

criterion for evaluating the quality of contact and mutual support. For example, during a session, the patient might begin talking about a work-related problem (figure). As they explore it, an emotion linked to a past relationship might arise with greater intensity (new figure), temporarily shifting the work problem to the ground. If the therapist sensitively follows this shift, encouraging the patient to explore the new emotional figure, and then they return together to the work issue with a new perspective, a fluid figure/ground dynamic is observed. In contrast, if the therapist rigidly insists on maintaining focus on the work issue, ignoring the emerging emotion, a rigidity in the figure/ground dynamic might be observed, signaling a potential interruption in the contact process.

- The *quality of mutual synchronization*: are the patient and therapist in tune, or do they struggle to "find the rhythm" together? This criterion refers to the ability of the patient and therapist to attune emotionally. Synchronization implies a reciprocal connection, where both participants seem to "feel" each other, both verbally and non-verbally. For example, during a session, the patient might recount a painful event in a restrained tone, and the therapist, maintaining an empathetic and calm expression, might spontaneously slow their breathing or use a lower, more soothing voice. This non-verbal resonance signals mutual emotional synchronization, creating a bond that facilitates contact. Conversely, if the patient expressed frustration in an agitated tone and the therapist immediately responded with a detached interpretation, without acknowledging the expressed emotion, a lack of synchronization might be observed, which could hinder emotional connection and slow therapeutic progress. Mutual synchronization is one of the most important indicators of the quality of the therapeutic relationship.

The discussion of relational diagnosis continues to be the subject of debate among various authors, offering new perspectives and insights (Sampognaro, 2014).

As emphasized by Wollants (2012), a key figure in the relational rereading of Gestalt therapy, every psychopathological disorder stems from an alteration in the reciprocal relationships between the person and their environment. Distress is not only about the intrapsychic dimension but is the result of a dynamic that is continuously co-constructed between the individual and the environment. However, in my opinion, it is important to note that a psychopathological disorder is not exclusively relational in nature; it also involves the internal psychic structures of the ground of the individual's experience. These internal structures interact with relational dynamics but cannot be reduced to them. For a complete Gestalt diagnosis, it is not enough to consider solely the figure of the current contact, i.e., the situation co-created by the organism and the environment; it is necessary to include the experiential background, that is, the relational style and contact patterns the patient has acquired from past experiences.

As we have seen, Perls, Hefferline, and Goodman, consistent with their phenomenological present-centered perspective, focus diagnostically on the structure of the current contact process rather than the type of individual character. However, despite this choice by the founders, I believe that diagnostic assessment cannot ignore the individual's developmental past and their repetitive perceptual and relational patterns, which are an integral part of the background of their experience. The diagnosis of the figure and that of the background are closely interdependent and enrich each other. In the current figure, we can recognize fixed and unaware patterns that belong to the background and that the person tends to repeat in different situations. At the same time, understanding the background helps us better understand the structure of the current figure.

It is important to be aware of the risk of excessively simplistic diagnostic readings of character that fail to grasp the psychological complexity of a person or neglect the ever-present relational dimension. However, it is essential to consider the patient's experiential background, i.e., the relational and characterological patterns developed throughout their life, which may influence the perception and dynamics of contact. When the experiential background prevails over the present reality, it can distort the perception of what is happening. Although every contact figure is co-created by the organism and the environment, they do not always participate in the same way or to the same degree. It is therefore crucial to assess whether a relational dynamic is more determined by the patient's character structure or by the therapist's actions. An example of how the character structure may distort the perception of the present emerges in the brief exchange that follows, where the patient's projective style becomes evident. The conversation takes place in a public setting, with the therapist and patient separated by a desk.

Patient (P): To tell you everything, I think you just made an "erotic transference" toward me.

Therapist (T): An "erotic transference"? How so?

P: By moving your hand toward your genitals.

T: And how was that for you?

P: Well, I won't hide it, it disturbed me, but I guess it's part of therapy.

As we have seen, the type of neurotic characters proposed by Perls, Hefferline, and Goodman is inadequate for describing the dynamics of the current contact process from a relational perspective, as it does not reflect the interactive and reciprocal aspect of these dynamics. However, despite these limitations, it represents a fundamental contribution to understanding and classifying the various dysfunctional contact styles within neurotic pathology. The characterology proposed by the founders remains a diagnostic model useful for describing the different types of neurotic experiential backgrounds. Therefore, it should not be overlooked but rather deepened and further developed, integrating it with a more relational and dynamic view that takes into account reciprocal interactions and changes occurring in the therapeutic process.

Notes

1 For a deeper exploration of the concept of narrative identity, see, among others, Bruner (1990), McAdams (1996), and Ricoeur (1991), who highlight the structuring role of language and storytelling in the construction of the self.
2 The quote has been translated from the Italian edition: Polster, E. (1986), "*Prigioniero del presente*", *Quaderni di Gestalt*, 2(3), 63–82. The original English edition is: Polster, E. (1985), "*Imprisoned in the Present*", *The Gestalt Journal*, 8(1), 5–22.
3 For a clear and detailed description of these mechanisms, see Robine (2013), who defines them as *flexions of experience*.
4 The term "*destroying*" should be understood, within the vocabulary of *Gestalt Therapy*, as part of the creative adjustment process, in which the organism exerts functional aggression to modify or de-structure aspects of the environment that hinder the satisfaction of a need. It does not refer to a destructive act in a pathological sense, but rather to an essential phase of the contact process. When this movement is inhibited, as in retroflection, the aggressive energy can no longer be directed outward and is instead turned inward, against the self.
5 Some authors have highlighted the inaccuracy of the expression "interruption of contact", as the contact process does not come to a complete halt but continues to occur to some extent.
6 In this regard, it is interesting to note that Westen *et al.* (2012), within the context of the classification system for personality styles and disorders, identified two fundamental neurotic styles – one hysteric-histrionic and the other obsessional – through the empirical analysis obtained using the Shedler-Westen Assessment Procedure-II (SWAP-II) and Q-Factor analysis.

References

Bruner, J. (1990). *Acts of meaning*. Cambridge, MA: Harvard University Press.

McAdams, D. P. (1996). *The stories we live by: Personal myths and the making of the self.* New York: The Guilford Press.

Perls, L. (1976/1997). Comments on new directions. In E. W. L. Smith (Ed.), *The growing edge of Gestalt therapy* (pp. 221–226). Highland, NY: The Gestalt Journal Press.

Perls, F., Hefferline, R., & Goodman, P. (1951/1994). *Gestalt therapy: Excitement and growth in the human personality*. Highland, NY: The Gestalt Journal Press.

Polster, E. (1986). Prigioniero del presente. *Quaderni di Gestalt, 2*(3), 63–82. (Original work published 1985, Imprisoned in the present, *The Gestalt Journal,* 8(1), 5–22).

Ricoeur, P. (1991). *Oneself as another* (K. Blamey, Trans.). Chicago, IL: University of Chicago Press. (Original work published 1990).

Robine, J.-M. (2013). Anxiety within the situation: Disturbances of Gestalt construction. In G. Francesetti, M. Gecele, & J. Roubal (Eds.), *Gestalt therapy in clinical practice: From psychopathology to the aesthetics of contact* (pp. 479–493). Milano: FrancoAngeli.

Sampognaro, G. (2014). La sofferenza della relazione come criterio condiviso: Co-creare una psicopatologia Gestaltica. *Quaderni di Gestalt*, 27(2), 9–30. https://doi.org/10.3280/GEST2014-002002

Spagnuolo Lobb, M. (2013). *The now-for-next in psychotherapy: Gestalt therapy recounted in post-modern society*. Milano: FrancoAngeli. (Original work published 2011 as *Il now-for-next in psicoterapia*, Milano: FrancoAngeli).

Spagnuolo Lobb, M. (2016). Self as contact, contact as self: A contribution to ground experience in Gestalt therapy theory of self. In J.-M. Robine (Ed.), *Self: A polyphony of contemporary Gestalt therapists* (pp. 261–289). St. Romain de Virvèe: L'Exprimerie. (Original work published 2015 in French).

Westen, D., Shedler, J., Bradley, B., & DeFife, J. A. (2012). An empirically derived taxonomy for personality diagnosis: Bridging science and practice in conceptualizing personality. *American Journal of Psychiatry*, *169*(3), 273–284. https://doi.org/10.1176/appi.ajp.2011.11020274

Wheeler, G. (1991). *Gestalt reconsidered: A new approach to contact and resistance*. New York, NY: Gardner Press.

Wheeler, G. (2016). The future of the self: Reflections on contact, development, and the "sub-systems of the self" in Paul Goodman. *Gestalt Review*, 20(3), 235–256.

Wollants, G. (2012). *Gestalt therapy: Therapy of the situation*. Thousand Oaks, CA: Sage. (Original work published 2008, Turnhout: Faculteit voor Mens en Samenleving).

Chapter 8

The Concept of the Field in Gestalt Therapy

Developments and Implications[1]

8.1 Introduction

The concept of the *organism/environment field* is a central element in Gestalt therapy. It represents a fundamental conceptual framework for understanding the interdependence between the individual and their environment. This is a highly valuable theoretical principle with significant and contemporary implications. However, in the psychological domain, the term *field* is a subject of debate, as it takes on different meanings depending on the theoretical perspectives adopted. Even within Gestalt literature, the concept of the field has never reached a single, universally accepted definition. Authors have offered a range of interpretations, at times even conflicting. My aim is not to propose a synthesis, but to underline this plurality as a source of richness in the literature rather than a limitation.

Staemmler (2006), for example, considers the field as the phenomenological world—that is, the totality of subjective experience—distinct from the trans-phenomenological, physical, and social world. According to Staemmler, the concept of the organism/environment field proposed by Perls *et al.* (1951/1994) involves a "category mistake," as it conflates the phenomenological world with the trans-phenomenological one. Similarly, Robine (2004) conceives the field as a subjective phenomenon. In his view, when two people meet, one cannot speak of a shared field, as each person's field remains distinct from the other's. While they both create a common experience, each individual lives it differently. Parlett (1991), on the other hand, argues that in the relationship between two people, there are neither two separate fields interacting with each other nor two distinct individualities that remain isolated. Instead, each individual, through interaction with the other, actively participates in the co-creation of a shared field, as we will explore later. Philippson (2017) considers the field to be a physical reality, just as the contact process itself is physical, always involving the body. If we conceive of the field merely as a subjective experience, Philippson asks, how can we explain the *full contact* that occurs in an intimate encounter between two people, where, for a certain period, the distinctions between their subjectivities dissolve? Francesetti (2014), drawing on Hermann Schmitz's *New Phenomenology*, describes the field as a *quasi-thing*: something ephemeral and elusive, neither purely subjective nor

DOI: 10.4324/9781003726753-9

objective, perceptible as an atmosphere, a vibration, a sensory and affective resonance.[2] Spagnuolo Lobb (2013, 2018) considers the field a phenomenological given, meaning the experience of encounter and friction between two alterities: the organism and the environment. Although the perception of this process is subjective, the process itself constitutes a unitary totality, co-created by the organism and the environment. In line with Parlett (1991), the author conceives of the field not as a merely subjective reality but as an intermediate dimension, in which the separation between subjectivity and objectivity is transcended. Furthermore, Spagnuolo Lobb links the concept of the field to that of the contact-boundary. The field represents the unity of organism and environment, while the contact-boundary refers to movements within the field itself, namely, the interaction between organism and environment. From this definition of the field, Spagnuolo Lobb (2017) develops the concept of *aesthetic relational knowledge*, understood as the therapist's embodied sensitivity and perceptual attunement to the field, which allows them to gain a deep understanding of the "dance of reciprocity" in which the patient's experience unfolds (Spagnuolo Lobb, 2019).[3] The first section of this paper, which does not claim to resolve the issues related to the definition of the field concept, will briefly examine the concept itself in Lewin (1935, 1936) and in Perls *et al.* (1951/1994). Subsequently, I will analyze the evolution of the Gestalt concept of the field, highlighting the shift from an individual-centered perspective to a relational one, which characterizes the more recent developments in Gestalt therapy.

In the following sections, I will delve deeper into certain aspects and implications of the Gestalt notion of the field. To this end, I will examine it through three closely interconnected themes: *holism*, *ecology*, and *quantum mechanics*. In my view, these paradigmatic categories can help us better grasp the richness and relevance of the field concept in Gestalt therapy, as well as enable its historical and cultural contextualization.

The findings of modern physics, particularly Einstein's theory of relativity and quantum mechanics, have challenged the reductionist, mechanistic, and deterministic assumptions of classical physics and, more broadly, of Western scientific thought. Alongside this paradigm shift, a new interdisciplinary orientation emerged in the early 20th century, inspired by a holistic and ecological vision of the world (Capra, 1982). It is within this cultural shift that I will attempt to contextualize the Gestalt concept of the field.

8.2 From the Individual Field to the Shared Field

The concept of field originates in physics, particularly in the classical unified field theory, developed by Michael Faraday (1791–1867) and James Clerk Maxwell (1831–1879). According to this theory, two or more interacting bodies are not separate entities exerting action at a distance on each other in an empty space; rather, they are part of the same totality, the same physical reality: the field, which mediates their interaction.

It was Kurt Lewin who introduced the concept of the field in psychology, with the aim of explaining the complexity of the reciprocal interactions between internal and external forces that determine human behavior. According to Lewin (1935, 1936), in order to understand the behavior of an individual at a given moment, it is necessary to consider the totality of the internal and external conditions acting upon the person at that precise instant. In other words, behavior is not determined by past psychological events, but by the overall psychological situation of the present—that is, by the totality of coexisting and interdependent psychological events. For Lewin, then, the individual and the field are an inseparable unity, and behavior is a function of that field.

Although Lewin's field theory represents an important historical inspiration for Gestalt therapy, it is crucial to emphasize that the concept of field elaborated by Perls, Hefferline, and Goodman diverges from it radically. Their elaboration marks a crucial shift from an abstract perspective to a phenomenological and relational one.

For Lewin, the field is an abstraction: a conceptual tool for mapping the psychological and environmental forces that influence the individual. It is a dynamic model that describes the totality of internal conditions (needs, motivations) and external ones (environment, social relations), useful for understanding behavior but distinct from the individual's direct experience.

In Gestalt therapy, by contrast, the field is lived experience: the dynamic reality that emerges in the *hic et nunc* from the interaction between organism and environment. It is not a theoretical model observable from an external standpoint, but something perceived, felt, and co-created in each moment of contact. As Perls *et al.* (1951/1994) put it in a well-known passage of *Gestalt Therapy*:

> The definition of an animal involves its environment: it is meaningless to define a breather without air, a walker without gravity and ground, an irascible without obstacles, and so on for every animal function. The definition of an organism is the definition of an organism/environment field.
>
> (p. 35)

This view underscores that organism and environment are integral parts of a single indivisible whole, and that experience is not reducible to the individual but emerges at the contact boundary.

This shift from abstraction to lived experience marks the transition from a causal-deterministic model to a phenomenological and relational one, making the field in Gestalt an active and directly experiential component of therapy, rather than a mere system of external forces.

Although Perls, Hefferline, and Goodman moved the concept of the field in a more experiential direction, their perspective remains centered on the individual's relationship with the environment, without fully integrating the reciprocity of relational dynamics, as we saw in Chapter 1.

A further step toward a truly relational conception of the field was taken by Parlett (1991), who describes the field as a triadic configuration, emphasizing its co-created nature. What one person does or says becomes the context that, in part, determines what the other will do or say next. Parlett (1991) writes,

> It is a bit like the abstract expressionist painter who places one splodge of paint in the middle of an empty canvas. This begins to structure the field, begins to organise that particular reality. The second application of paint has to be in relationship to the first. And as the painter adds new splodges, the opportunities to do something totally different become more difficult. There are fewer degrees of freedom. The field has become formed, it has been gestalted.
>
> (p. 76)

Similarly, two interacting individuals influence each other and, step by step, co-create the shared field.

Stern (2004), a psychoanalyst in many ways close to Gestalt therapy, goes beyond Parlett's description of field co-creation, emphasizing that a fundamental characteristic of every interaction is intersubjectivity, that is, the sharing of experiences between two individuals. Each person intuitively participates in the other's experience, perceiving their thoughts, emotions, and intentions. Stern also adds that, in certain moments, particular shared experiences occur: this happens when two individuals live the same experience at the very moment it unfolds, achieving a sort of interpenetration of their minds. These experiences, particularly significant in therapy as well as in life, are what Stern calls *moments of meeting*. However, it should be noted that, for Stern, the *intersubjective field* is essentially a mental phenomenon, whereas in Gestalt therapy—as we will see in the next section—the field is understood as the inseparable totality of mind, body, and external world.

At this point, I propose the following description of the field as it manifests between two people in contact: a dynamic play, or an "interference pattern"—to borrow a term from physics—arising from the interaction and interpenetration of one person's experience with that of the other. Within this field, each individual, starting from themselves and in relation to the other, continuously creates and recreates, moment by moment, their own field in relation to the other's. Each person perceives reality from their own perspective and generates a field, which in turn interacts with the field of the other.

The notion of a separate *ego* dissolves into the dynamic interplay of interacting and interpenetrating fields. An effective metaphor for this dynamic is that of two currents of water that initially flow separately but, upon meeting, begin to intertwine, influencing and transforming each other. Each current's movement modifies the flow of the other, creating a single watercourse, with new trajectories, vortices, and continuously evolving directions.

Similarly, in the encounter between two individuals, their experiences do not remain separate but rather intertwine within a shared field, which is not merely the sum of the two experiences but a new, co-created reality in constant transformation.

We speak of individual subjectivity for convenience, but the individual exists only within a shared field. Individual and relational dimensions are not separate—they constitute a single reality: the field.

In line with this evolution toward a fully relational and situated conception of the field, Gutjahr (2024) proposes a radicalization of the field-centered paradigm, arguing that "contact is the first reality" and that every therapeutic experience is grounded in real resonances that traverse the co-created field. In his proposal, Gestalt therapy must emancipate itself from the implicit individualism still present in many interpretations, adopting a deeply sociopolitical and embodied perspective. Gutjahr's approach highlights how the dynamics of hyper-individualism and commodification of the self, typical of liquid modernity, produce alienation and desensitization—thus directly questioning the ethical and clinical responsibility of the therapist in the co-creation of the field.

8.3 Holism

The Gestalt field theory is situated within a holistic vision of human nature and reality. The term "holism" was introduced by Jan Smuts (1870–1950), a South African politician and philosopher, author of *Holism and Evolution*, published in 1926. Holism refers to a theoretical approach based on the idea that the whole is greater than the sum of its parts. In *Ego, Hunger and Aggression* (1947/1969), Perls, who had embraced some of Smuts' fundamental ideas, strongly recommended reading the South African thinker's book.

According to the authors of *Gestalt Therapy*, who state "the irreducible unity of the sociocultural, animal, and physical field in every concrete experience" (Perls *et al.*, 1951/1994, p. 15), holism characterizes our immediate perception of reality. Our primary experience of the world, the first evidence, consists of wholes of experience that take shape as unified structures. What we immediately perceive is the whole. Only later do we decompose this totality into its constituent parts. From a phenomenological perspective, only these wholes of experience are real. Anything else is merely an abstraction. Even the concepts of organism and environment are abstractions: "We speak of the organism contacting the environment, but it is the contact that is the simplest and first reality" (Perls *et al.*, 1951/1994, p. 3).

The term "abstraction" comes from the Latin *abstrahere*, meaning "to draw out," to separate. The process of abstraction, which consists of isolating a measurable and reproducible part from the complexity of reality, is at the core of the scientific method and represents a fundamental tendency of our culture. We live in a world where abstraction tends to prevail over concrete, immediate, and lived experience, in some way becoming more real than the reality from which it was extracted. As a result, we end up mistaking the map for the territory, confusing our abstract models with reality itself. Perls, Hefferline, and Goodman recognize that abstraction is both useful and essential. If we want to reflect on totality, we cannot help but separate its parts. However, an excess of abstraction becomes dysfunctional, as it reflects "a rigidity of training and functioning, a verbalizing-character that indeed cannot attend to the whole series, except in theory" (Perls *et al.*, 1951/1994, p. 43).

According to Perls, Hefferline, and Goodman, in moments of "good contact," that is, moments of fullness of experience, we experience the fundamental unity of mind, body, and the external world. The authors write (Perls *et al.*, 1951/1994, p. 169): "The self, aware in middle mode, bursts the compartmenting of mind, body, and external world." The mind does not exist as a reality separate from the body, nor is the body something distinct from the mind; it is a lived body, a direct experience inseparable from our awareness. Similarly, the reality of the things around us does not exist independently of us but rather emerges from contact. We are our lived body in actual contact with the surrounding world. Mind, body, and external world are not independently existing realities but rather complementary and inseparable aspects of the contact process. The separation between these three concepts is an illusion, arising from the primacy of the deliberate attitude of the self over spontaneity, a primacy that characterizes the epidemic neurosis of our society. This separation leads, on the one hand, to a reduction in the sense of the body as part of the self and, on the other hand, to the perception of the external world as foreign to the self.

Since Descartes, modern science has contributed to the division between mind, body, and the external world. In the dominant scientific models, derived from his teachings, it is assumed that a physical, objective world exists first, within which life eventually develops. Later, with the evolution of an increasingly complex nervous system, consciousness, that is, the mind, emerges, reaching its highest level of development in humans. This mind, situated within the body, experiences the body itself and the external world.

This view of reality, based on the clear distinction between *res cogitans* (the mind) and *res extensa* (matter), a distinction inherited from Descartes, has been challenged by quantum physics. Although Gestalt therapy and quantum physics belong to different domains of knowledge, interesting analogies can be identified in how both conceive the relationship between subject and reality. There is a notable resonance between the concept of field in Gestalt therapy and the vision of reality that can be coherently extrapolated from experimental data in quantum physics. According to this perspective, mind and matter, subject and object, constitute an inseparable unity (Sabbadini, 2017). For quantum physics, which will be discussed again in the final section of this chapter, the world is not something determinable and existing in itself, independently of who observes it. For example, the position of an electron is described as a probability cloud that, only at the moment of observation, and due to the very act of observing, "collapses" into a precise point. The state of the particles we observe is, in some way, determined by the act of observation itself. Curiously, in a similar way, Perls *et al.* (1951/1994, p. 153) state: "What is important to notice is that the actuality contacted is not an unchanging 'objective' state of affairs that is appropriated, but a potentiality that in contact becomes actual." In both Gestalt therapy and quantum mechanics, self and world, subject and object, emerge together in the act of experience.

The holistic perspective contrasts with the reductionist one, which holds that the whole can be fully understood by reducing it to its component parts. From a reductionist standpoint, psychic phenomena are considered reducible to neurophysiological processes. Today, most neuroscientists believe that psychological processes are nothing more than epiphenomena, that is, secondary products of neural processes occurring in the brain. However, the brain is a physical organ that operates according to causal connections, which cannot be different from what they are. The brain, in itself, is not conscious, does not reflect, does not choose, does not assign meaning, does not take responsibility, and does not perceive beauty. It merely responds to physical stimuli from the environment according to cause-and-effect laws. Perls *et al.* (1951/1994, p. 147) write: "It is not the self of the organism as such." For the authors of *Gestalt Therapy*, the creative activity of the self is not a product of the brain. The self is a function of the organism/environment field. Psychological processes do not occur within us, inside the brain. Rather, they are relational processes that take place not inside the organism but at the contact-boundary within the organism/environment field. For Gestalt therapy, the psychological phenomenon is a relational event and, as such, is not reducible to neurophysiological data. Perls *et al.* (1951/1994, pp. 150–151) write: "Organic physiology, thoughts and emotions, objects and persons, are abstractions that are meaningful only when referred back to interactions of the field." Neurophysiological processes constitute the material conditions underlying psychological processes, but they do not coincide with them. They are abstractions which, as such, possess no psychological meaning. The field perspective of Perls, Hefferline, and Goodman is clearly anti-reductionist.

8.4 Ecology

I use the term *ecology* here, referring in particular to the meaning attributed to it by Gregory Bateson (1972, 1979) when he speaks of the *ecology of ideas* or the *ecology of mind*. An anthropologist and biologist, Bateson defined the *ecology of mind* as his original theoretical perspective, aimed at identifying the formal and structural similarities between biological, cognitive, and social systems, in order to demonstrate the existence of a fundamental relationship between mind and matter. Bateson strongly affirms the monistic nature of reality. In his view, the mind, understood as a set of complex cybernetic networks—of which the individual mind is only a part—is intrinsic to matter, immanent in nature. Thus, Bateson attempts to rebuild the bridge between culture and nature that characterized ancient forms of wisdom but has been progressively abandoned by modern Western man. Bateson's ecological perspective consists precisely in this attempt to overcome the division between man and the world, in order to regain an original condition of wisdom and harmony.

Perls, Hefferline, and Goodman also observe that in prehistory there was no clear separation between human beings and nature. Our ancestors, they claim, did not dominate nature but rather lived in symbiosis with it.[4] With the development of civilization, we have distanced ourselves from this harmonious union with the world. Civilization, with its legacy of institutions, symbolic structures, and conventions—what we call culture—has distanced us from direct contact with reality, progressively replacing our natural functions and stifling our creativity. The relationship with nature has thus become instrumental, as Perls *et al.* (1951/1994, p. 47) write: "Natural resources are 'exploited': that is, we do not participate with them in an ecology, rather we use them, a safe attitude that leads to much inefficient behavior. We 'conquer' nature, we are the masters of nature. And persistently, conversely, there is the strain that it is 'Mother Nature'."

Bateson's holistic and ecological approach presents numerous points of contact with that of Perls, Hefferline, and Goodman.[5] I will limit myself here to briefly indicating some common ideas and themes:

- the holistic perspective, which asserts the impossibility of considering the individual in isolation, separated from the environment, situation, or context in which they are embedded;
- the critique of Cartesian dualism and the mechanistic view of science;
- the search for an epistemology not reducible to reductionist materialism;
- the denunciation of fundamental dichotomies that characterize Western culture and hinder the integration of experience: reason and emotion, individual and society, mind and body, mind and matter, and so on.

Another point of contact can be identified, at least in some respects, in the concept of *self-regulation*, present in both the Gestalt model and Bateson's approach. According to Perls, Hefferline, and Goodman, self-regulation consists of a kind of intrinsic wisdom that the organism possesses regarding its own needs and its ability to choose, within the environment, what can satisfy them. From a relational perspective, *self-regulation* implies a shared wisdom through which the organism and the environment cooperate, integrating each other's needs. Perls, Hefferline, and Goodman describe this interfunctioning between organism and environment, which can be defined as *field self-regulation*, through the example of the mother–child relationship:

> The child's anguished cry is an adequate communication; the mother must respond to it; the infant needs fondling, she needs to fondle; and so with other functions. The delusions of omnipotence (to the extent that they exist and are not adult projections), and the rages and tantrums of infinite abandonment, are useful exhaustions of the surface-tension in periods of delay, in order that interfunctioning can proceed without past unfinished situations. And ideally considered, the growing apart of the infant and the mother, the disruption of this field into separate person, is the same as the increase of the child in size and strength, his growing teeth and learning to chew (and the drying up of the milk and the turning of the mother to other interests), and his learning to walk, talk, etc. That is, the child does not learn an alien reality, but discovers-and-invents his own increasing reality.
>
> (Perls *et al.*, 1951/1994, p. 46)

Bateson speaks of self-regulation in relation to systemic processes. He seeks to understand the functioning of the mind and living beings through general systems theory and cybernetics. A system is a set of elements in reciprocal interaction. Bateson considers the human being—both physiologically and psychologically—the society, and the ecosystem as cybernetic systems, capable of self-regulating through autocorrective feedback processes. According to Bateson, in the absence of external interferences, such processes naturally tend toward a harmonious functioning of the whole. On this point, he writes: "Left to itself, any large piece of Creatura will tend to settle toward tautology, that is, toward internal consistency of ideas and processes" (Bateson, 1979, p. 206). Here, the author describes *Creatura*, the world of mental processes, as a self-regulating system that naturally tends toward balance and coherence.

What hinders systemic self-regulation, according to Bateson, is our rationality, which he defines as *conscious purpose*—a concept corresponding to the deliberate mode of the self described by Perls, Hefferline, and Goodman. Bateson believes that *conscious purpose*, to which Western culture attributes excessive importance, represents an obstacle to wisdom and grace. In his view, these can only be achieved through awareness of the systemic and interconnected nature of reality. Similarly to Perls, Hefferline, and Goodman, Bateson argues that to counteract the predominance of rationality, it is necessary to give space to experiences such as poetry, artistic creation, play, love, and dreams. To these, he adds contact with animals and nature, as well as the deeper aspects of religious experience. Bateson (1972, p. 438) writes: "These are all activities in which the whole individual is involved"; and later adds that they "are areas in which more of the mind is active than mere consciousness would admit" (Bateson, 1972, p. 447). Bateson's words echo the description that Perls, Hefferline, and Goodman give of the *spontaneous self*, understood as the mode of total and integrated functioning of the self, as opposed to its partial functioning modes. Bateson defines as *non-purposive* what Perls, Hefferline, and Goodman call *spontaneous*. Thus, in Bateson, we find—though expressed in a different language—the distinction between intentionality and spontaneity, a fundamental aspect of Perls, Hefferline, and Goodman's theory of the self. The latter, moreover, express an ecological vision akin to Bateson's when they state: "A child is in confluence with his family, an adult with his community, a man with the universe" (Perls *et al.*, 1951/1994, p. 232). We are part not only of the field we directly experience but also of a broader field, consisting of society and the entire ecosystem. We function best when we are in harmony with others, with the community in which we live, and with the world as a whole.

Despite the affinities between Bateson's ecological perspective and that of Perls, Hefferline, and Goodman, there is a substantial difference between the two. Bateson bases his worldview on cybernetics, a paradigm that surpasses mechanism by integrating a systemic and relational perspective, with the aim of reconciling holism and reductionism. The very notion of self-regulation highlights the gap between the Batesonian and Gestalt approaches. For Bateson, systemic self-regulation is not a teleological process attributable to the intentionality of consciousness, but rather the result of information exchanges and feedback mechanisms. Bateson's cybernetic and systemic epistemology differs markedly from the phenomenological epistemology of the Gestalt approach.

8.5 Quantum Mechanics

According to the predominant reductionist perspective in neuroscience, sooner or later we will be able to fully explain mental functions based on neurophysiological processes. Assuming this is possible, such an achievement still seems far off. At present, purely deterministic explanations of psychological processes appear inadequate.[6] It almost seems as if our brain transcends itself. How this might happen remains an unresolved question, one that quantum mechanics might perhaps shed light on.

Today, we know that the universe is not governed solely by deterministic causal laws. The universe is creative: its creativity arises from unpredictable processes and chaotic dynamics of disorder. Ilya Prigogine, Nobel Prize winner in Chemistry in 1977, defined *dissipative structures* as those systems in which order emerges spontaneously and unpredictably from disorder.[7] In nature, order can arise spontaneously from chaos.

We owe to quantum physics, which studies the infinitely small world of elementary particles that make up the atom, the discovery that the universe possesses a certain degree of indeterminacy. According to Heisenberg's uncertainty principle, we cannot precisely determine both the position and velocity of a particle simultaneously, not due to limitations in our measuring instruments, but because of the intrinsic properties of matter at the quantum level. Quantum mechanics has challenged the deterministic view of classical physics, introducing a new paradigm for understanding natural phenomena.

It is not my intention here to delve into the principles of quantum physics, nor do I have the expertise to do so. I will limit myself to briefly mentioning the astonishing reality revealed by the study of the subatomic world.

One of the most puzzling quantum phenomena is what is known as *entanglement*. In simple terms, *entanglement* describes the profound connection between two correlated elementary particles, A and B, such that any change affecting particle A has a measurable effect on particle B, regardless of the distance between them. Mysteriously, the two particles appear to maintain an instantaneous connection, even when placed vast distances apart—a phenomenon that Einstein famously called *spooky action at a distance. Entanglement*, which has received numerous experimental confirmations in recent decades, represents one of the greatest challenges for modern physics, as it calls into question our traditional understanding of space, time, and causality.

The discoveries of quantum physics have highlighted the limitations of a purely objective conception of the universe, challenging our very notion of matter. Reality is not something entirely objective and measurable; it is not composed of separate material objects. Consider, for instance, the dual nature of particles, which can manifest as waves or corpuscles depending on experimental conditions, or the fact—already mentioned—that the measurable properties of particles are determined only at the moment of measurement. In this sense, quantum reality is not entirely objective but is, in part, dependent on the interaction with the observer. The advent of quantum mechanics has redefined the principles of classical physics, showing that it represents only a limiting case valid for the macroscopic world. Consequently, we can no longer regard classical physics as the ultimate foundation of scientific knowledge.

In light of these discoveries, the universe appears as an immense field in which everything is interconnected. These interconnections seem to be instantaneous, unlike cause-effect relationships, which are necessarily limited by the speed of light. Reality is not composed of separate entities that, like billiard balls, interact in space and time according to causal laws. Each phenomenon can be interpreted as the local manifestation of an immensely vast field, in which all particles are interrelated in ways that challenge traditional notions of space and time. This vision of quantum physics presents striking analogies with Eastern wisdom traditions, which affirm the interconnectedness of all things and the fundamental unity of the universe (Capra, 1975; Sabbadini, 2017).

Quantum mechanics applies to the subatomic realm, while in the macroscopic world in which we move, classical physics predominates. However, the idea that quantum effects may also manifest at the macroscopic level is now widely discussed. Recent research has shown that various biological processes, such as the sense of smell, bird navigation, and photosynthesis, could be influenced by quantum phenomena. According to a particularly intriguing line of study, even the physical processes underlying mental activity might involve quantum mechanisms. If confirmed, this hypothesis could offer new perspectives on the understanding of the relationship between mind and brain.[8]

At this point, we can no longer take for granted that human experience is solely the product of neurophysiological processes governed by the laws of classical physics. We cannot remain anchored to a purely materialistic vision of reality. Perhaps psychological processes could be better understood through quantum mechanics rather than in terms of classical physics. In truth, we still know little about quantum processes occurring at the microscopic level, among atoms and molecules, and even less about how they might influence macroscopic systems, such as biological organisms, cells, and brain processes. We cannot rule out that, in the future, quantum physics discoveries may prove relevant in various fields of knowledge and healthcare. We might even discover that the field created in the encounter between two people is a quantum phenomenon.

Rightly so, Latner (1983, p. 88) writes,

> It is apparently the case that the differences in the practical applications of classical and modern physics are measurable only with tiny particles travelling nearly the speed of light. [...] Well, maybe the fabric of the universe encompasses all of it, and we large bodies moving at slow speed can feel the tug of

those faster, smaller particles. Maybe the immeasurably moving things that happen in therapy – the inchoate knowledge, and hints of things I could not have known, the sudden intimacy and shared experience – maybe these are also parts of a world as palpable as our material one, and confluent with it. Maybe we are, after all, small, fast-moving bodies, and this is the speed of light.

8.6 Concluding Reflections

The concept of the field places Gestalt therapy within a historical, cultural, and epistemological framework that reflects a holistic-ecological view of reality. This approach aims to overcome both the deterministic and mechanistic view of classical science, as well as the utilitarian attitude of indiscriminate exploitation of the environment, which causes the progressive depletion of natural resources and disrupts socioeconomic balances.

Perls *et al.* (1951/1994, p. 322) highlight one of the greatest difficulties for modern man, which is understanding and accepting that "the organism and its supporting world must be in intimate contact for growth, development and life." This principle of interconnection between organism and environment, which forms the basis of Gestalt therapy, offers a crucial perspective in addressing contemporary global challenges. The environmental crisis, which now permeates every aspect of daily life, is rapidly approaching a point of no return, with the imminent risk of irreversible catastrophes. Scientists warn us that the epidemics of recent decades are, in part, the result of disruptions in ecosystems.

In response to these global challenges, it is necessary to profoundly rethink the relationship between man and the environment, moving beyond competitive and utilitarian models of a productivity-oriented culture that is based on the accumulation of goods, the indiscriminate exploitation of resources, and the reification of the human being. Equally essential is rethinking the relationship between individuals, viewing the human community as a "fraternal community," to use the expression of Perls, Hefferline, and Goodman, founded on cooperation and solidarity.

This cultural shift, which stands as an indispensable ethical-existential choice, represents the only way to prevent future generations from inheriting a desertified and uninhabitable world. In this context, Gestalt therapy, with its concept of the organism/environment field, can offer a significant contribution by promoting the development of new modes of relationship and fostering the creation of a more respectful and equitable society.

The purpose of this work is not to provide a new definition of the Gestalt concept of the field but rather to contextualize it within a historical, cultural, and epistemological framework, highlighting its development and contemporary relevance. Although it has been the subject of extensive discussion, the concept of the field still holds a wealth of implications that remain to be explored. I hope that this work, while not claiming to cover every aspect of the concept of the field, can stimulate reflections and new developments, both within the field of Gestalt therapy and in the broader social and cultural reflection.

Notes

1 Previously published in *Quaderni di Gestalt* (2020), 33(1), 57–73. Originally published in Italian. https://doi.org/10.3280/GEST2020-001005
2 Roubal and Francesetti (2022) have more recently defined the phenomenal field as the horizon of possibilities offered by the specific situation in the present moment. The field determines which experiential phenomena can emerge in the here and now and which, instead, remain in the background. It is a *quasi-objectified* reality that influences the arising of phenomenal events. By way of example, Roubal and Francesetti present the following scenario: at a gathering of friends, the field will foster the emergence of joy, jokes, and laughter, while at a funeral vigil, it will give rise to sadness and stillness.
3 Roubal and Francesetti (2022) distinguish three perspectives on therapeutic change in Gestalt therapy: *mono-personal*, *bi-personal*, and *field perspectives*. In the *mono-personal perspective*, the therapist directly intervenes to facilitate change in the patient's experience. In the *bi-personal perspective*, change emerges from the co-created relationship between patient and therapist, conceived as two distinct subjects. Finally, in the *field perspective*, change results from spontaneous processes that transcend individual subjects, emerging from the dynamics of the shared phenomenological field. Roubal and Francesetti place the metaphor of dance—used by Gestalt authors such as Spagnuolo Lobb (2016, 2017) to describe the therapeutic contact process in a reciprocal framework—within the *bi-personal perspective*. However, a deeper analysis suggests that the "dance steps" model proposed by Spagnuolo Lobb may be better understood within the *field perspective*. This model involves the application of *aesthetic relational knowledge*, a form of immediate and spontaneous knowing of the field through the senses, which allows the therapist to navigate their actions within the complexity of the therapeutic encounter. From this perspective, change is seen as a unified process involving both patient and therapist. Therefore, the *dance steps* model, with its emphasis on *aesthetic relational knowledge* and the spontaneous dynamics emerging within the phenomenological field, can be considered representative of the *field perspective* in Gestalt therapy.
4 The relationship with the environment that characterizes primitive cultures has been defined by the French anthropologist Lucien Lévy-Bruhl (1857–1939) as *mystical participation*. The primitive perceives everything around him as animated and feels deeply connected to it.
5 The existence of a harmony between Goodman's and Bateson's thought finds anecdotal confirmation in the testimony of Susan Goodman (2016), daughter of Paul Goodman. In an interview dedicated to various aspects of her father's life, the author highlights the friendship and mutual esteem that, at a certain point in their lives, connected the two intellectuals. She also recounts how, during their conversations, they were in perfect agreement and fully satisfied with their mutual exchange of ideas.
6 Today, cognitive neuroscience is generating increasing interest and enthusiasm both within the scientific community and among the general public. However, neuroscientific research, primarily based on neuroimaging techniques and *cognitive subtraction*, still has significant limitations that are often overlooked (Legrenzi & Umiltà, 2009).
7 See Prigogine and Stengers (1984).
8 The idea that mental processes have a quantum basis has been proposed by scholars such as Roger Penrose and Stuart Hameroff (*Orch-OR theory*), but it remains highly controversial and lacks definitive experimental evidence. According to this hypothesis, consciousness would emerge from quantum vibrations in microtubules, protein structures found within neurons. Consequently, it would not derive solely from synaptic connections between neurons, as traditionally hypothesized in neuroscience models, but would also be influenced by quantum processes occurring within the neurons themselves. The Orch-OR theory was initially formulated by Penrose (1989) and later expanded in more

detail in Penrose (1994). The hypothesis was subsequently developed further in collaboration with Hameroff in a comprehensive review article (Hameroff & Penrose, 2014).

References

Bateson, G. (1972). *Steps to an ecology of mind.* New York, NY: Ballantine Books.

Bateson, G. (1979). *Mind and nature: A necessary unity.* New York, NY: Dutton.

Capra, F. (1975). *The Tao of physics: An exploration of the parallels between modern physics and Eastern mysticism.* Boulder, CO: Shambala Publications.

Capra, F. (1982). *Turning point: Science, society, and the rising culture.* New York, NY: Bantam Books.

Francesetti, G. (2014). Dalla sintomatologia individuale ai campi psicopatologici: Verso una prospettiva di campo sulla sofferenza clinica. *Quaderni di Gestalt*, 27(2), 31–56. https://doi.org/10.3280/GEST2014-002003

Goodman, S. E. (2016). Growing up with Paul Goodman: Reflections on his life and work. *Gestalt Review*, 20(1), 7–32.

Gutjahr, L. (2024). *A field-centred approach to Gestalt therapy: Agency and response-ability in a changing world.* London: Routledge.

Hameroff, S., & Penrose, R. (2014). Consciousness in the universe: A review of the Orch-OR theory. *Physics of Life Reviews*, 11, 39–78. https://doi.org/10.1016/j.plrev.2013.08.002

Latner, J. (1983). This is the speed of light: Field and systems theories in Gestalt therapy. *The Gestalt Journal*, 6(2), 71–90.

Legrenzi, P., & Umiltà, C. (2009). *Neuro-mania. Il cervello non spiega chi siamo.* Milano: Il Mulino.

Lewin, K. (1935). *A dynamic theory of personality.* New York, NY: McGraw-Hill.

Lewin, K. (1936). *Principles of topological psychology.* New York, NY: McGraw-Hill.

Macaluso, M. A. (2020). Il concetto di "campo" in psicoterapia della Gestalt: Sviluppi e implicazioni. *Quaderni di Gestalt*, 33(1), 57–73. https://doi.org/10.3280/GEST2020-001005

Parlett, M. (1991). Reflections on field theory. *The British Gestalt Journal*, 1, 68–91.

Penrose, R. (1989). *The emperor's new mind: Concerning computers, minds, and the laws of physics.* Oxford: Oxford University Press.

Penrose, R. (1994). *Shadows of the mind: A search for the missing science of consciousness.* Oxford: Oxford University Press.

Perls, F. (1969). *Ego, hunger, and aggression: The beginning of Gestalt therapy.* New York: Vintage Books (Random House). (Original work published 1947).

Perls, F., Hefferline, R., & Goodman, P. (1951/1994). *Gestalt therapy: Excitement and growth in the human personality.* Highland, NY: The Gestalt Journal Press.

Philippson, P. (2017). *Topics in Gestalt therapy: Revisiting the field* (Vol. 1). Manchester: Manchester Gestalt Centre.

Prigogine, I., & Stengers, I. (1984). *Order out of Chaos: Man's new dialogue with nature* (translated by A. Toffler). New York, NY : Bantam Books.

Robine, J.-M. (2004). *Plis et Déplis du Self.* Bordeaux: Institut Français de Gestalt-thérapie. (Original work published 1977).

Roubal, J., & Francesetti, G. (2022). Field theory in contemporary Gestalt therapy Part Two: Paradoxical theory of change reconsidered. *Gestalt Review*, 26(1), 1–33.

Sabbadini, S. A. (2017). *Pilgrimages to emptiness: Rethinking reality through quantum physics*. Pari: Pari Publishing.
Spagnuolo Lobb, M. (2013). *The now-for-next in psychotherapy: Gestalt therapy recounted in post-modern society*. Milano: FrancoAngeli. (Original work published 2011 as *Il now-for-next in psicoterapia*, Milano: FrancoAngeli).
Spagnuolo Lobb, M. (2016). Gestalt therapy with children: Supporting the polyphonic development of domains in a field of contacts. In M. Spagnuolo Lobb, N. Levi, & A. Williams (Eds.), *Gestalt therapy with children: From epistemology to clinical practice* (pp. 25–62). Siracusa: Istituto di Gestalt HCC Italy.
Spagnuolo Lobb, M. (2017). From losses of ego functions to the dance steps between psychotherapist and client: Phenomenology and aesthetics of contact in the psychotherapeutic field. *British Gestalt Journal*, 26(1), 28–37.
Spagnuolo Lobb, M. (2018). Aesthetic relational knowledge of the field: A revised concept of awareness in Gestalt therapy and contemporary psychiatry. *Gestalt Review*, 22(1), 50–68.
Spagnuolo Lobb, M. (2019). The paradigm of reciprocity: How to radically respect spontaneity in clinical practice. *Gestalt Review*, 23(3), 234–254. https://doi.org/10.5325/GestaltReview.23.3.0232
Staemmler, F.-M. (2006). A Babylonian confusion? On the uses and meanings of the term "field". *British Gestalt Journal*, 15(2), 64–83.
Stern, D. N. (2004). *The present moment in psychotherapy and everyday life*. New York, NY: W. W. Norton & Company.

Index

For Product Safety Concerns and Information please contact our EU
representative GPSR@taylorandfrancis.com
Taylor & Francis Verlag GmbH, Kaufingerstraße 24, 80331 München, Germany

www.ingramcontent.com/pod-product-compliance
Ingram Content Group UK Ltd.
Pitfield, Milton Keynes, MK11 3LW, UK
UKHW022122190926
475702UK00013B/1601
* 9 7 8 1 0 4 1 2 1 3 3 8 3 *